MARTIN ELLIS JR.

Testimony Scrolls of Destiny

The Overcomer's Secret Weapon

GLORY RELEASE GLOBAL

I dedicate this book to the following:

To my lovely wife, Prophetess LaRonda Ellis, for being my partner in this journey of destiny. For being there with me through the ups and downs and for always praying for me. LU4E

To my wonderful mother, Dr. Winnetta Ellis, for instilling in me Christian values and for believing in me. You have always been one of my greatest role models.

To my spiritual father, Pastor Leonard H. Barber. Thanks for your time and for being an example of humility & love.

Contents

Preface   ii

Introduction   v

Chapter 1 : BEFORE WE WERE HERE   1

Chapter 2 : OUT OF ETERNITY WITH EXPECTATION   15

Chapter 3 : IT IS IN YOU   32

Chapter 4 : FIND & UNRAVEL   46

Chapter 5 : FAITH IS A TESTIMONY   58

Chapter 6 : THE HOLY SPIRIT HAS A TESTIMONY   71

Chapter 7 : JESUS CHRIST THE SCROLL OPENER   82

Chapter 8 : CIRCUMCISION OF THE HEART   97

Chapter 9 : PRAYER & FASTING   111

Chapter 10 : ASCENSION TO THE FULL SCROLL   130

Chapter 11 : WHAT IS ON OUR SCROLL? (PART 1)   148

Chapter 12 : WHAT IS ON OUR SCROLL? (PART 2)   160

Chapter 13 : OTHER SOURCES & INDICATORS   173

Chapter 14 : TYPES OF SCROLLS & CONCLUSION   188

About the Author   205

Preface

Background and Intention Of This Book

I have been doing ministry things for almost 25 years and have written many articles and have had unofficial books hanging around for many years. I have been shown that I would be an author and it has been prophesied to me from a number of prophetic voices. But now is the time to start the release within me with this book. This book will have a central theme around understanding and fulfilling the God given destiny in your life. It will touch a number of other topics that I would have loved to go deeper on but we have to stay at a high level overview. You might say there are many books on this topic. Why do we need another one? I am with you in this sentiment but apparently part of my destiny is to write a book about destiny. (laugh) I want to be obedient to the leading of the Holy Spirit even though I might think that this topic is supersaturated in the book market. There are billions of people on the earth and maybe I have been given a piece and a perspective that will be a blessing to a specific group of people. So I will trust God in that this book will bring revelation and aid in catapulting people in the will of God for their lives so that in the end they and myself can hear the words, "Well Done , good and faithful servant".

I just want to give a little background of how this book was composed and birthed in my heart to write. In the fall of 2020, many changes occurred in my life and the Lord launched me into a different phase of my life. It was a rebirth in a number of ways. I shifted from pastoring one work and was sent on assignment to be an assistant pastor with my spiritual father. I was given an opportunity from the senior pastor to minister for two consecutive Sundays at the church where I am now part of the leadership team. As I sought the Lord on what to teach or preach about. Two topics came into my spirit but "Destiny" was the first one I heard.

Only about a week before the prompting to teach on destiny, did I skim a book posthumously written by Neville Johnson that was not even complete that was surrounding the topic of Destiny. His son searched his hard drive and gathered some notes and compiled it as a small book. As I began to pray and dig into the scriptures about the topic, the Holy Spirit began to download something very powerful in me things I never heard or read. I began to see some scriptures jump out that I never seen or thought about in that way. It began to be so much that even as I was doing other things, the revelation just kept coming. It was as if the inward teacher would not stop talking. As I continued to hear things from the Holy Spirit, I would keep on just adding to my notes. It was so much that I realized that the whole two weeks would be used to be a series with 2 parts about Destiny and I would not even get to use that time for a second topic.

As I began to minister this series and tried to crunch this into 2 weeks, more revelation continued to come. The notes continued to grow. The congregation was really open and excited about the messages even to the point where the senior pastor asked that I continue for a third week. During these services, the atmosphere was charged with the presence of God and I witnessed great angelic activity and destinies and mantles revealed. It was amazing to watch the revelation from the Lord be a blessing to the people of God. As I pondered this and next steps, it was spoken in my spirit, to release this revelation as a book. Also, I felt a push and urgency from the Holy Spirit to write this book by early 2021 which is a small amount of time. I was told that this was the window that he ordained for this book to be released and it would be pivotal for the body of Christ for the move of God that he is bringing in upcoming years starting in 2021 and beyond. Writing this book has come with its joys but also with its share of spiritual warfare. During this period, my wife and I were sick with COVID-19 where my wife was hospitalized for a nice amount of time. Other attacks occurred from the enemy but I knew I had to persevere to release this book. I believe this book will speak to you from an eternal perspective of God's destiny for your life. It will also teach you how to pursue this in your journey as a believer. It will also release revelation of how to tap into the eternal weapon that the Most High has placed in your hands to be an overcomer and more than a conqueror.

Introduction

Through the ages of time, billions of people have lived and walked many paths in this earth. I am sure a great majority have pondered many questions in their mind. Questions like the following: Is there a God? Why are we here? What is the purpose of life? What is man really? Are we alone in this universe? I am sure I am not alone in wondering different questions like the aforementioned, when it comes to , as some would call, "the mysteries of the universe". I believe that the Most High God of the universe, even though we feel out of the know, has planted something deep within us that sparks a certain curiosity to ask these types of questions. The real question is what are you going to do with these questions? Will you be the one who sits on these questions and pursues nothing? Or will you be the one who pursues the answers with every part of your being and not be satisfied till things are revealed for you? The Most High is looking for such who have the mindset and passion to seek after the answers. The God of the universe is a God who is true to his promise that if you seek, you definitely find.

Some are under the impression that this life is just about surviving and if I keep my head down and just go through it without causing too much a stir, then I am doing good. But the truth is that God has sent his Son, Jesus, to come that we might have life and life more abundantly. Even the notion that accepting Jesus is just about getting to heaven when you die is a pretty watered down version of the true gospel of the kingdom of God. God the Father has an intention to everything he has created and through his foreknowledge he has assigned to everything a purpose. It is his goal that in this life (not after we die) that everyone will live an abundant and overcoming life according to his design, destiny, and purpose.

We Are Called To Overcome

Revelation 12 (KJV)

10 And I heard a loud voice saying in heaven, Now is come salvation, and strength, and the kingdom of our God, and the power of his Christ: for the accuser of our brethren is cast down, which accused them before our God day and night. 11 And they **overcame him** *by the blood of the Lamb, and by the* **word of their testimony**; *and they loved not their lives unto the death.*

The above scripture talks about the goal of the power of Christ which is to bring salvation, strength, and the kingdom of God is our lives. Verse 12 begins after the theme of salvation to talk about the victorious body of Christ walking in overcoming power over the enemy. The theme of being an overcomer shows to us that there are things in life that we must rise above, conquer, and be victorious over. I highlight this point to encourage that the name of the game is not just to survive or look to barely make it into heaven all beat down , busted, and disgusted. But the aim is to walk and become an overcomer in Christ because quite frankly there is a war going on. Some might not realize that they need Christ in their lives. Some may understand the importance of Christ but may wonder how to move from being a slave to sin to being an overcomer in the kingdom of God. There might also be a company of people that mostly know about the power of the blood of Christ on some level but miss the other key to overcoming the enemy. I believe as we look deeper in the given scripture that there is a secret weapon revealed that we should utilize in our lives to be a victor and not a victim.

It is so imperative that we get the revelation in our hearts and minds that we are called to overcome. Once that is established as a foundation to our everyday lives, then we must also realize that the God of this universe placed us here not just to call us to something but has provided the needed tools to obtain that calling. As mentioned earlier, to overcome implies that we are warring against an enemy who is trying to stop us from reaching a certain goal. And if we are in a war against an enemy , we must identify the weapons and tools that have been given to win the war. The Lamb of God, Jesus Christ, has been crucified before the foundation of the world for us before he manifested in the earth. (Revelation 13:8) And from this sacrifice, the blood of Lamb has been made available to blot out the record of our sins and transgressions before God Almighty to put us in right standing before him. This is important and power against the enemy. But with any good fighter (boxer), it is good to have a combo to knock out the opponent. Per the scripture in Revelation 12, we have been the other weapon along with the blood of Christ which is "the word of their testimony".

Word of Testimony Misunderstood

This term of "the word of their testimony" is the foundation of this book. It is my mission to elaborate based on this phrase to equip the body of Christ with such a powerful weapon that the enemy won't be able to stand against us. The major problem is that we who know the scripture do not have the right perspective when thinking on this clause of words of "word of their testimony". The first misconception is surrounding the word "Word". A lot might focus on the word "Word" and think that if we alone have the scriptures and begin to profess the scriptures that we have the power alone in the scriptures (Word) to defeat the enemy. Of course this helps on some level. But in John 5:39, it reveals that if you search the scriptures, some people think that in them alone is eternal life. But the goal of the scriptures is to point you to Jesus Christ. So the "Word" is more than just scriptures it is actually Jesus Christ. (John 1:1) It is very interesting that this scripture in question is the book of the bible that is about the "Revelation" (unveiling) of

Jesus Christ. We must allow the scriptures (Word - logos) to point to Christ himself (living Word) to reveal the right now alive word just for our lives personally (Rhema Word).

The second misconception that is sometimes applied is around the word "testimony". There is a connotation that testimony always means that a person went through a trial or test and when they came through that situation, then that is their "testimony". Some might also say if a person has a "testimony", then that person has a story to tell. In other words, that person has witnessed or seen some things. Also, before it was popular to start church services with praise and worship, it was prevalent for you to start service with prayer and "testimony" service where people will stand up and give testimonies about how God worked in their lives. These services were powerful while people were expressing the goodness of God and glorifying his name. But this type of testimony is not what Rev. 12:11 is referring to. If we used some of the applications of "testimony" that I just mentioned, then we are not using the correct context. The context is that the body of Christ has been given a weapon that they can use while the war is going on to overcome the enemy. If we assume that a testimony is what we have at the end of victory, then that does not match having a testimony "during" the war. Some might say "Well I am claiming by faith the testimony" before it happens. I can go along with that. But what is faith based on? It is based on the sure word of God that has already been declared. I submit to you the premise that the testimony that should be in our hands as believers is something that was placed there before the war got good and started. We will discuss this more in later chapters.

The third objection is about "whose" testimony if referred to here. You might hear some say that is the testimony and witness of God's word and that when you boil it all down, this is referring to God's testimony. And where I believe this is true on some level, the phrase is "word of **their** testimony". The possession of the referenced testimony is under the ownership of the believer. This testimony and word and declaration of this testimony should be aligned as a witness of God's own testimony. If there is a witness of the testimony of God for your life, then what consists in this testimony? The testimony of God concerning you that you need to witness and align to is his thoughts and plans concerning you. There is a song based on scripture that says , "Whose report will you believe?" We will believe the report (witness, testimony) of the Lord". Hence, the word of our testimony deals with the will of God, purposes, and destiny for our lives.

We All Have An Eternal Destiny

This leads us to this statement, the Most High God of the Ages had you in mind in the beginning with very specific details that he preordained that you should walk in to bring you to an expected end. We all as spiritual beings and creations of God have an eternal destiny that was assigned to us before we came into this earth. There are particular records in the heavens and the earth that has a mapped out destiny for you. Our mandate is to seek this out and to fulfill this scroll of destiny with our names on it. This leads us to the title of the book that God wants us to know and handle the "testimony scrolls of destiny".

My Prayer

Our God which is in heaven, Abba Father, I pray that your will be wrought in this book. May this book contain words that are ordained from heaven with the assignment to remove scales from eyes and impart wisdom from above. Father, I pray that everyone who reads this book will be filled with the spirit of revelation and wisdom in the knowledge of you and that the eyes of their understanding be enlightened that they may know the "hope of your calling". That they may know their destiny. I pray that you open their hearts and that these words be planted deep and produce the harvest of destiny being fulfilled in their lives. I pray that a new hunger to pursue you be in their belly. I pray that they hear the call from eternity to please you and live for you. In Jesus name, Amen.

* * *

Chapter 1 : BEFORE WE WERE HERE

* * *

There are many theories out there from many perspectives on what is the meaning of life and when does life begin for a human being. As long as the earth is in place till the fullness of the kingdom of God covers the earth, there will be many opinions on this matter. But we are walking in an hour where it is God's intent for his people to come together of one mind, one truth, and one Lord and King. This is imperative because this is important for the believer to walk in truth and for a company of believers to walk in truth together in one accord. When this happens, the world will see something awesome in manifestation. But also, the body of Christ will defeat the enemy and overcome because together they are utilizing the right weapons that God has placed in their hands. This has been the plan of the Most High from the beginning for there to be an overcoming people for his name and Kingdom on the earth.

If this has been the heart of the Father from the beginning, then he also had us in Him and in his mind from the foundation of the world. Some might think that life began for an individual when the sperm connected with the egg in the womb. Some , especially who are for abortion, believe life began when a person is delivered out of the womb. From the perspective of the bible, we are a tripartite being which is spirit, soul, and body. There is a strong inclination for us to think more about the body side of us in this physical realm. But I want you to know that your spirit man is more real and eternal than your physical body. We are a spirit being that is having an earthly experience. I am sure there are other thoughts, even some conflicting, on this around the world, but God wants us as believers to know his truth based on his Word. Let's look into the scriptures.

In the Beginning we were in the Father

Romans 11 (KJV)

*36 For **of him**, and through him, and to him, are all things: to whom be glory for ever. Amen.*

In the above scripture , the "him" referenced in the context of the 11th chapter of Romans is God Almighty himself, our Heavenly Father. In the beginning before things like the earth, the stars, and the moon were created, our Father had a plan for creation. He was very intentional, strategic, and very detailed about what he wanted to accomplish. Nothing was just done on a whim or on a spur of the moment action. His ways are higher than our ways and his thoughts are higher than our thoughts. And part of his ways and thoughts were that he will birth something in him, release it out of him, mature it through him, and receive back to him. The scripture above clearly points to our origin. We are not just the product of our earthly father's and mother's DNA coming together. Neither are our earthly parents being the source and beginning of our being. We were definitely created in the realm of eternity "of" the Father himself containing his nature, light and breath.

2

Ephesians 1 (KJV)

3 Blessed be the God and Father of our Lord Jesus Christ, who hath blessed us with all spiritual blessings in heavenly places in Christ:

*4 According as he hath chosen us **in him** before the foundation of the world, that we should be holy and without blame before him in love:*

Before we established in Romans 11, that we are "of" the Father. And just in case some might want to say that "of" is not necessarily "in", let's continue with the above verses. In Ephesians 1, it is explained that we were chosen "in him". Someone might say that we are chosen to be "in him" after we give our lives to Christ. But the verse continues to say "before the foundation of the world". We were "in him" before the foundation of the world and was chosen with a purpose and destiny. It goes on to reveal that we were chosen to be holy and without blame "before him" in love. There is a difference between being "in him" and being "before him". Another way I would phrase it is that we were in him, then chosen to come out of him to later be before him holy (set-apart) and without blame. This is in harmony with the scripture in Romans 11, that relates that we first are "of him" so we can "through him" end up back "'to him". The whole goal is to be one big circle where God and his Christ is the beginning and the ending.

The many who are very acquainted with this physical earth realm, in reality within, are spiritual beings who have spent time in the person and mind of the Father. We were not some little particle with no knowledge of being and just existing in a glob of nothingness. But we were children of the Most High with a consciousness towards the Father. We had personalities and spent time with the Father and each other. Quite plainly, before we came on earth, we existed in the Father. You might wonder why I am so sure of this. The answer to this is because it was revealed to me during a time of prayer over 20 years ago.

Three Vision Experiences

This is not something I have talked too much about in the past because I did not hear anyone talk of such things back in the 1990s. In 1997, a while after I rededicated my life back to Christ, I began to experience God and the spiritual realm in a new way. So many different things were happening to me and I did not know anyone at the time experiencing these types of things and I did not know where any reference to any of these things were in the scriptures either so I just took note and recorded some of things as I continue to seek clarity. Thanks to the Father that now others have come forward with revelation, visions, dreams, encounters, and experiences that have aligned to some of things I have experienced in this spiritual journey.

First Vision

Well here is one of the vision experiences I had in 1997. Before I go into the experience, I just want to confirm that I was not intoxicated, high, or smoking anything. I was in prayer and was taking to a place in the spiritual realm where all around me was mostly pure white with outlines of gray and powered by light. I saw a beach or shore landscape with sand but nothing was in other colors. What was shocking was I could see as far as my eyes can see, these little (the best way I can describe it) gingerbread men looking beings. I saw what seemed like millions of them. They were in groups and I was one of them. I could feel the connection to the Most High but also can feel a oneness and connection to all the other beings. We enjoyed one another in fellowship and we played together. We could do many things like fly and position ourselves in many different ways. We could stack up on one another and make shapes and even glide and walk on the water. The experience ended because the presence of the Father came on the scene and we all stopped what we were doing so we could fellowship with him. I came to myself before I could see the Father. Through prayer and seeking the Lord concerning this, it was later revealed to me that this was us before we came into the earth.

Second Vision

This vision experience I also had in 1997. During prayer I was taken to a scene above the earth around the stars. I could see the earth beneath with the land and the seas. Then I saw the huge hand of the Father holding a huge container like a can. And from that moment, my point of view is now that I am in the can. I am not alone. I am in there with millions of souls. Once again, we were all connected. There was a certain sound and frequency that resonated from us. It was a sound of praise to the Father and a sound of expectation and thankfulness of being chosen to be released out of the container for a certain purpose. All of the sudden, you heard the hand open the container. It sounded like a soda can was being opened and the pressure inside was being released. Then the hand began to pour us out one by one in his timing out of the container into the earth. Once again through prayer and seeking the Lord, I was told that this represented mankind who was ordained before the foundation of the world with an assignment that was according to the counsel of his own will to be released into the earth.

Third Vision

This third "vision experience" is a little hard to share because when it occurred I was in awe of what I just witnessed. I was in shock and denial of the whole experience for a while because I could not wrap my mind around it. I am only sharing this because the Lord has instructed me to share this

5

encounter. This was not part of my first draft of this chapter. In the fall of 2007, my wife worked nights as a nurse but we had a 6 month baby at home. I would take the night shift of watching over the little guy. With him being so young, he did not always sleep during the night so sometimes I would be up. When this happened, I would just either pray or sing praises to God. One time while I was during this, I was holding my son in my arms trying to rock him to sleep and it was like we both went into a new dimension together. In this place, my son still looked like a baby and was still in my arms. The next part is what shocked me. He began to speak to me with a very elaborate vocabulary. Remember this is a six month old who has not even accidentally said "Da Da" yet.

As he speaks, he proceeds to say some interesting things that were mind blowing to me. He says "Hello Martin, I am glad that I got an opportunity to talk to you like this since most babies don't get this privilege". He goes on to tell me that he was sent from above for a very special purpose and destiny. He also elaborates that we knew each other before we came to earth and we agreed that I would be his father in the earth to help guide him to his destiny. He then encourages me to stay true to my call and to always remind him of his. And from there we were back in my bedroom and he was sound asleep. I sat there like "What just happened?". I was convinced I was being part of a trick and someone would jump out and say , "We got you". Before this, only my wife and some of our kids knew this story. I shared this because even though we have to be careful with the visions and dreams we have, we have to pay attention to them , no matter how bizarre, in case God is trying to get something to us. Thankfully, I believe as we go further, we will be able to see scriptures in the bible that aligns with this position of revelation.

Declaring the End From the Beginning

Isaiah 46 (KJV)
9 Remember the former things of old: for I am God, and there is none else; I am
God, and there is none like me,
*10 **Declaring the end from the beginning**, and from ancient times the things*
that are not yet done, saying, My counsel shall stand, and I will do all my pleasure:

We were created by an awesome God and best believe there is none like him. He is a God of tremendous foreknowledge. When you break down that word, you have "fore" and "knowledge". It means he had a knowledge or intimate knowing of details before he moved forward in execution. As noted, Christ is declared the beginning and the ending. God's hope is for your ending to look like what was declared in the beginning. As above in the verses, he declared the end according to his own counsel and pleasure in the beginning. We are used to thinking of things in a linear (line) type of thinking where we start at one destination and end up at another. But God wants us to think of things in an eternal and circular perspective outside of time and space where the end and beginning touch. The only way for us to make sure that our ending looks like what the Father has declared already is for us to be "through him" and abide in Christ. Christ is the beginning and the ending because in him the ending and the beginning are the same. If we are in Christ who is the author and finisher of our faith, then we can align with God's declaration for our lives from the beginning. (We will talk more about this in later chapters.)

He Knew Us Before We Were Here

It has been discussed earlier that we were "of him" and "in him" during the beginning. We were not fragments of energy or balls of light just floating around freely with no trajectory. We were spiritual beings with a mind, emotions, communication ability, and the power of choice. There was communication going on with the Father, his Son, and also with each other. There was a real fellowship and intimacy going on within the Father. Information, knowledge, revelation, and God's will was being expressed to all of us. It was an atmosphere of learning, joy, peace, and praise in the realm of eternity. We definitely had an intimate knowledge of the Father and his plans and us as his children, he knew oh so very well. It was an awesome moment in eternity but the Father had a purpose for us as well as the earth to mature us in his glory. Let's look at two scriptural examples that demonstrate how well the Father knew us and that he called us and set us apart for certain purposes.

Jeremiah

Jeremiah 1(KJV)
5 **Before** I formed thee in the belly **I knew thee**; and **before** thou camest forth out of the womb I **sanctified** thee, and I **ordained** thee a prophet unto the nations.

In this example with Jeremiah, we see that God "knew" Jeremiah before he was even in his mother's womb. He knew Jeremiah before his parents came together to create him in the natural world. This word "knew" is the Hebrew word (yada) which means to know by experience, to recognize and be acquainted with. This is the same Hebrew word that was used to describe the intimate knowing of Adam with Eve before Eve became pregnant with

8

Cain. In eternity, Jeremiah and the Father had an intimate experience and knowledge about each other before Jeremiah's spirit was placed in the womb on earth. Some might think well this is an isolated incident just for Jeremiah and maybe some other special people. But this is not the case because our God is not a respecter of persons. In the same way he knew Jeremiah before he was in his mother's womb, he knew each and every one of us.

God not only knew us but just like Jeremiah, he set us apart and ordained certain things in our lives. In Jeremiah's case, he was sanctified and selected to be a prophet to the nations. We might have been elected by his grace to be a prophet to the nations like Jeremiah, but through God's foreknowledge and counsel within himself concerning us, we have all uniquely been ordained for something. This election of grace did not happen after you were born. This selection did not happen the day you might have given your life to Christ. This ordination did not happen after you walked with Christ for a while and proved yourself faithful. This knowing and declaration of who you are was established in the "before".

Paul

Galatians 1 (KJV)
*15 But when it **pleased God**, who **separated me** from my mother's womb, and **called me by his grace**,*
*16 **To reveal his Son in me**, that I might preach him among the heathen; immediately I conferred not with flesh and blood:*

So now, let's review Galatians 1 where Paul is testifying concerning his own life and calling. We mentioned before in another scripture that God does things according to his own counsel and his own pleasure. Paul says in verse 15, that when it "pleased" God, he was separated or set apart from his mother's womb. Then it goes on to say he was called or elected by God's grace for a specific purpose of Christ being revealed in him. This is important because everything we are tasked to accomplish must be done by Christ. We can do all things that the Father has ordained through Christ who strengthens us. Is it just me or is this very similar to Jeremiah's experience? Jeremiah was not alone in this and Paul was not special by being the only one. We all were known by the Father in the Father before we were sent to earth for God's mission.

So with these two examples, there is a pattern that emerges that reveals God's working in us from all eternity. The pattern is as follows:

1. Before in the womb, the Father knew us intimately and had purpose for us.
2. By being placed in the womb, he separates and sets us apart from the other spirit beings eternity to release us into the earth
3. While being In the womb, he calls our name and stamps us with his purpose to ordain us for a work and destiny

All this happens before any first cry outside the womb or even any confession of Christ. This is why the scripture says interestingly enough in the same chapter of the book of Romans that we started this book chapter with, (Romans 11:29) that gifts and callings come without repentance. Many think of this in terms of our repentance which I believe holds true that we are given callings and giftings before we walk in repentance. But the other side of the coin is God's repentance. Repent means to "change your mind". And the other perspective of this scripture is that through God's election he gave callings and giftings without even having to change his mind because he trusted his own wisdom, foreknowledge of you, and counsel. Our Father which is in heaven is the only wise and awesome God and we knew him in eternity and he trusted and faith in us to send us to earth.

A Book (Scroll) Written About Us

Psalms 139 (KJV)
*14 I will praise thee; for I am **fearfully and wonderfully made**: marvellous are thy works; and that my soul knoweth right well.*
*15 My substance was not hid from thee, when I was made in secret, and **curiously wrought** in the lowest parts of the earth.*
*16 Thine eyes did see **my substance**, yet being **unperfect**; and **in thy book all my members were written**, which in continuance were fashioned, when as yet there was none of them.*
*17 How precious also are thy thoughts unto me, O God! how **great is the sum** of them!*

It amazes me that we live in a world where most of academia agrees that there was a big bang that created this world and it eventually evolved into what it is today without the help of any superior deity, intelligence, plan, or intention. Oh well, that does not make any sense to me when you look at how amazing, detailed, and interconnected all creation is. Verse 14 of the above passage says we are fearfully and wonderfully made. This testifies that we are not just coincidence or some accident of nature. We are here deliberately by a God who is so powerful and infinite in his attributes and abilities. We are the marvelous handiwork of the Most High God.

Nothing of us was hidden from God's eye and nothing caught him by surprise because he saw our substance. Our substance is everything that we are, why we are, who we are and what we are. This automatically raises in my spirit Hebrews 11:1 that says faith is the "substance" of things hoped for. We were made with substance embedded with things that we should hope for. We were not perfect yet but had to go through an experience and process on the earth to come into perfection. For to be brought into glory and perfection, we too had to suffer some things. This is the key we fashioned with a substance with a code within that was filled with his thoughts of us to bring us to the summation of greatness. He saw us and placed his substance with his intentions in us so we can be what he declared from the beginning.

The beautiful part is that this destiny, this embedded code was not forced upon us. It was through his knowing of us and our knowing of him that we came into covenant with each other for us to be sent to earth. Through his knowing of us, he elected us by his grace for a certain destiny. And it was through our knowing and love for him that we agreed to this before we came into the earth. Let's draw our attention to verse 15, it says that we were "curiously" made or wrought in the lowest parts of the earth. God's design to bring us to maturity was presented with a destiny. Through our love and curiosity we agreed to an adventure and quest on earth to become overcoming sons. Because Christ the Lamb of God was slain before the foundation of the world, we knew the plan of salvation as well. Can you all say with me? "It is a beautiful setup".

Now, I will focus on the main point I want to get across in this section which is highlighted in verse 16. God in his strategic and purposeful mind, wrote a book with our name on it. That is why when Revelation talks about the white throne judgment it says the "books" were open. Our book details his plan for our life detail by detail and it is our charge to align with the details in that book. This book as the verse relates, holds all our members. It outlines every specific part of us so much that even the hairs on our head are numbered. And it is written by him before we were placed on the earth as the verse ends with "when as yet, there was none of them". This book was written before we came here and there is a record of this book in heaven with the Father.

As we move forward, even though this scripture uses the word "book", I will begin to use the word "scroll". The reason is because a book contains many pages. Pages can be seen scrolls made out of paper. Hence, a book consists of many scrolls joined together to tell a story. As the scripture says, "How great is the sum of them". The book that he has written of us, is the sum of many scrolls containing many details about destiny in the earth. This is why the name of the book is entitled "Testimony Scrolls of Destiny". There are many scrolls that make up the book. Or if you want to, you can look at our book in heaven as one long scroll. This long scroll linked to us holds the testimony of the Lord that outlines our destiny.

Testimony of the Lord

2 Timothy 1 (KJV)
*8 Be not thou therefore ashamed of **the testimony of our Lord**, nor of me his prisoner: but be thou partaker of the afflictions of the gospel according to the power of God;*
*9 Who hath saved us, and **called us with an holy calling, not according to our works, but according to his own purpose and grace**, which was given us in Christ Jesus **before the world began**,*

The testimony or witness of the Lord is a powerful thing and something that we should not be ashamed of. It is more than just saying I have accepted Christ as my savior but it is a whole package of a lot of things. It consists of more than he saved us so we won't go to hell. But he also called us with a holy (set apart) calling. This calling is not based on any of our works. It is by grace that was a gift given us before we came here on earth. This gift of grace and destiny was given to us according to his own purpose and also with a ram in the bush. For Christ the Lamb of God was slain before the foundation of the world that he might have the preeminence to the church. So that through Christ and in Christ , we may fulfill the testimony of the Lord sanctioned for our lives. Once again, our goal is to accept the sacrifice of Christ so we know what is the testimony or report that the Lord has spoken over us from the beginning. Oh may our pursuit be to know what is on the testimony scrolls that were specifically assigned for us.

13

Prayer

Heavenly Father, may your grace be upon all who read this book. May the revelation that we were in the Father ring loudly in their hearts. May they see the infinite wisdom and amazing love you had towards us. And may they be drawn to you even more. As they draw towards you , draw nigh them in their journey to rekindle the relationship that they had with you in the "before". May they follow the pattern of Jesus with the cry in their heart that they may know the glory that they had before in you. May this hunger pulsate in every part of their being in Jesus name.

Chapter 2 : OUT OF ETERNITY WITH EXPECTATION

* * *

Oh what a glorious call that the Most High of heaven has bestowed to mankind. We have been wonderfully and fearfully made for great things. These things that he has ordained for our lives has been in the mind and heart of the Father since the beginning. He is so very patient to see his mind and intention play out through the course of time. Our identity of spiritual beings more than being a physical presence has a plethora of implications. Before our grand appearance on earth, we existed. And not only did we exist, we were sent here from the Father packaged with something to impact the world. In the previous chapter, we discussed who and where we were before we came to the earth. But now we will begin to shift to , on a high level, what was revealed to us and what type of package we were tasked to deliver to this world.

An Expected End

Jeremiah 29 (KJV)
11 For I know the thoughts that I think toward you, saith the Lord, thoughts of peace, and not of evil, to give you an expected end.

The above passage is a very important scripture and one that has been quoted many times. It gives us hope and it speaks to the heart and intent of the Father which is key. It gets me all excited and happy just thinking about the fact that I was not put here to aimlessly wander in a trajectory of life with no direction or expectation. The creator of all creation who sits on the throne of glory is not just sitting there with vanity in his mind, but his mind has a knowing of the thoughts that he thinks towards us. Not only that, but what type of thoughts does he have towards us? Some think because of what they are going through and what they see around the world that God has it out for them and he hates them. Some people think of God like a cold and disheartened individual who we see on reality tv shows and movies when a group of people are placed on a deserted island with no resources as an experiment to see how it all plays out.. No, no, no, my friend, it is quite the contrary.

The God whose thoughts and ways are higher than ours has a great capacity of focus and love concerning us. His thoughts are not evil like a mad evil scientist but his thoughts are geared towards an expected end. This is not a science or social experiment. God in his foreknowledge already knows the precise end he has destined you. His mind is not wondering about you from many different directions with uncertainty but he "knows" already what he thinks of you and what your expected end should be. And because he trusts in his own counsel, he is at peace with it. He knows and understands things at a frequency that we don't. He is infinite in his wisdom and knowledge.

The vastness of his capacity is so great that he has written a very detailed

16

book (scroll) , alluded to in Psalms 139, that was and is outlined with the finer details of your life and destiny before you even came on the earth. This ultimate record and book of your life is in the heavenly realm. The God of faith, can you believe it, has an expectation for your life. There is a destination, an expected ending point, he wants to bring you to through this earthly journey we call life. The details on your scroll for your life are plentiful. Believe that.

A scripture that speaks to me so deeply is in Psalms 8. The question of "what is man" is asked. Then it goes on to say that God is not only mindful of man but also visits him as well. I can feel the preach in me coming up in my spirit. If God is mindful of us, then that means his mind is "full" of us. Not just a stray thought here and there, but an unending flow of thoughts that if it could be possible to fill an infinite God's mind, it comes close to it. Also, we are not stranded here alone, but he visits man by his Spirit, his instruction and the guarding of his angels. He has branded us and charted us with an expected end and also strategically placed tools to place in our hands to ensure that we reach the finish line.

Charted For Glory

Things are charted and mapped out for our pilgrimage here on earth. That is why the bible points out that our perspective should be to see ourselves as pilgrims or strangers passing by on this earth. We are not originally from this earth, we are visiting from another source. Have you ever thought to yourself that I am not from this earth? Or maybe you thought I don't feel like I belong here. You feel you are connected to something that is bigger or higher than this realm of the earth. It drives you to search it out. Some look for it and find things like drugs, alcohol, fame, fortune, and the list goes on and still feel unfulfilled. I believe this is why some experience things like depression and thoughts of suicide because they know I was once connected to a certain source and need to be reconnected. Not realizing the whole time that we were born out of heaven for and with a purpose and Jesus Christ is the connection that links us back to that source.

As I ponder on the word "charted", it makes me think about a charter bus. I begin to imagine a person coming up with a vision to gather friends and family and plan out in detail an itinerary with specified stops and destinations. This imagination becomes a plan and then the plan becomes a reality. To move to reality, now this person needs a mode of transportation, passengers, a driver, funding, and an expected end. We were in the Father (imagination) and he wrote a book (scroll) about his thoughts for us (plan) and release out of eternity to manifest a reality. We are the passengers of the charter bus of life funded by the blood of Jesus driven by the Holy Spirit as we hold in our hands the itinerary (scroll) with an expectation to reach certain attractions of a trip designed by the Father. Oh the dream and expectation he has for us.

If there are no kinks in the plan, then things go smoothly. But unfortunately, we know that is not the case most times. In the technology arena, when a new product or software is being created, there must be a testing of quality that occurs before it goes to market. When testing happens, one stream of testing is called the "happy path". This is when you test the scenario of when everything flows with no objections, issues, or errors. But a great designer and tester is one who anticipates the other "not so happy" paths to program and test for those as well. Our Father in heaven is a master builder and strategist and has taken in account our personality, infirmities, failures, twists, and turns in the story he has written for us. It is our duty to align with him and find our charted "happy path".

Romans 8 (KJV)

28 And we know that all things work together for good to them that love God, to them who are the called according to his purpose.

29 For whom he did **foreknow**, he also did **predestinate** to be conformed to the **image of his Son**, that he might be the firstborn among many brethren.

*30 Moreover whom he did predestinate, them he also **called**: and whom he called,*
*them he also justified: and whom he **justified**, them he also **glorified**.*

The happy path of God that he has charted for us leads to bring us to an
expected end with him in his glory. Yes!!! You have been mapped out to reach
a mark of a joint heir with him on his throne. We, as children of the Most
High proceeded out of the father with his intent to cause us to mature as sons
of the Kingdom in his perfection. He has already made certain proclamations,
adjustments, and allowances for us before he sent us on this course for glory.
In God's foreknowledge of us, he has already (past tense), predestinated,
called, justified, and glorified us. He has assigned a destiny of sonship for us
before we came here and called us by his Word in the beginning. Then we
were justified by the blood of the Lamb that was slain before the foundation
of the world and he reserved for us a glory waiting for us as we overcame
the world through his Son. The charted happy path for us has a happy and
glorious ending.

From Good to Perfect

There might be a question in one's mind of if we were in the Father already
and if he wants to return unto him, why release us out of himself just to
return again? This is a good question. In short, the children who leave and
return won't be the same as if they left. There are two references that stick
out to me in the bible. One is in James 1, that says "every good gift and every
perfect gift comes from above". The other reference is found in Romans 12,
that says we need to present our bodies as a living sacrifice so we can prove
what is that "good, acceptable, and perfect will of God". It is implied that
God himself has two categories of things in heaven. One level is "good" and
the other is "perfect".

The direction of the kingdom of God is that of increase, knowledge, and expansion. It is his pattern and way to create something at one level with the intent for it to expand, grow and mature to a better level. His creation at its beginning is termed "good" but his goal and purpose for some of his creation is to upgrade through experience and testings to the level of "perfect". In Genesis, God said let there be light and there was light and he saw that it was "good". Then we see other things created and it was declared that God saw that it was good. Everything that God created was good but some things were not in its completed or "perfect" state. This pattern also holds true with mankind. In the Father, in his mind, we were good but he wanted to bring us to an expected end which was "perfect". So we finally see Adam on the earth and he is "good" but he is not "perfect" and in his proving, he was found wanting and fell. Thanks be to God. This did not catch him off guard for he already had a perfect plan of Christ as the sacrifice.

When we are born into this earth, we are born as babies and through the right training and nutrition we grow into mature adults. It is the same in the spiritual realm as well. When created in the Father, we were babies, and needed the right nutrition and training ground called earth that would mature us through trials, tribulation, and suffering to bring us to perfection. Our Father is not just good but he is good and perfect. Even Christ as the first begotten Son of the Father learned and matured in his experience of coming to earth and suffering. Hebrews 5:8 declares that even though he was a Son, he learned obedience by the things he suffered. Christ was even proven by his journey on earth as to increase in his level of perfection and obedience to the Father.

Jesus Christ declares in the gospels, that there is none "good" but the Father. So then that causes an inquiry of how God is able to declare something as good. It is because he sees his substance or intent in that thing so it then in his eyes is designated as "good". Perfection is the maturity of that thing to be formed fully into that he intended to be. This is why Jesus in the gospels at times encourages us to "Be ye perfect, even as your Father in heaven is perfect". With the genetic material of God Almighty through us when we are born again of his Spirit, the aim is to be changed into the same image and likeness of Jesus Christ. Can you imagine the Father looking at you and instead of seeing you as a baby, he sees himself while you reflect as the express image of his person? With mankind being children of the Most High and carrying the DNA of God, there is an expectation to move from the state of "good" children to "perfect" mature sons.

A Testimony From Eternity

John 1 (KJV)
*1 **In the beginning was the Word**, and the word was with God, and the word was God*

In the realm of eternity, in the beginning, was the Word. That Word which was and is Christ, was released from within the Father as a separate being who was "with" God. But in his being, he was so much in oneness. likeness and alignment with all that God was, he was God. As the book of Hebrews declares, he is the express image of the Father. He proceeded out of the Father as the Word. We all know before a "word" can be released, there must first be an image, thought, and intent within. He is the first begotten released from the loins of the Father. And because he embodied the full likeness of the Father, by him and for him were all things made. And from the releasing of the first begotten, it started a chain reaction for all of the whole of creation to be manifested out of the mind of the Father through the Son.

And us, being also spiritual entities within the Father, before the foundation of the world, we were eyewitnesses of the declaration and releasing of the full image, thoughts and intent of the Father encapsulated in entirety in the Son. In the Son, is contained the fullness of the Godhead. We in the Father beheld pieces of this fullness. As the plan of the Father was being declared and unfolded, we saw assignments, destinies, purposes, callings by

21

the election of the grace of God. In line to the title of this book, I want us to ponder on the word, testimony. What is a testimony? It is an eyewitness account or perspective of something that has already happened. While the fullness of the Word was manifested outside of the Father, the many mini words of the complete big logos Word wrote books and scrolls in the realm of eternity. We were eyewitnesses of this and therefore our spirit man holds a testimony.

In us, is a record, witness, and perspective that only we could have of this awesome declaration in the beginning. The beginning started with the Word proceeding and being birthed from the Father containing the fullness of all the desires, purposes, and pleasures of the Father. In spirit thought form, we were still in the Father with the rest of creation waiting to be pulled out of eternity through the Son. Everything had a timing and an order to be released and manifested. We saw some things. We heard some things. We experienced some things in that realm. We all have our own unique piece and perspective from our experience with the Word in the beginning. We are individually holding pieces of the testimony of eternity that when brought together tells the full story, heart, and intent of the Father.

Here is where things get interesting. Eventually, the angels were created and beheld on some level part of the intents of God. We received what we needed to know to fulfill our assignment and the angels received what they needed to know. Everything was on a need to know basis but the angels knew that part of their purpose was to be servants to the heirs of salvation. So they comprehended the plan of salvation on some level and that there will be heirs. Guess who was one of those angels. You already guessed it. Lucifer himself, the anointed cherub, one of the highest of the high in the rank of angels, was not pleased with this. From there a plan to be like the Most High and be an enemy of the purposes of God went into effect. A war was started and we are in the middle of that war. This is why this book is so important in these times because the scripture we started with lets us know that we overcome the enemy by the blood of the lamb and the Word of our testimony. We have a testimony out of eternity that we came to earth with. May we come to this knowledge and wield this eternal power weapon to defeat the enemy.

Agreement With the Beginning

I believe that the scriptures are saying more than one thing. That through God, there are multiple dimensions of the revelation he can bring to light through one scripture. Through his Spirit, who is the discerner and teacher of the Word, one scripture can speak to us from different perspectives and become inexhaustible in its feeding of our spirit man. I bring this up because you can see a scripture and think you have the fullness of what God wants you to get from it, but as you shift in life, you can come back and see something new as the Spirit reveals. Let's look at the following scripture.

1 John 2 (KJV)
*7 Brethren, I write **no new commandment** unto you, but an old commandment which ye **had from the beginning**. The **old** commandment is **the word** which ye have **heard from the beginning**.*

The context of the scripture is the commandment to love your brothers, sisters, and neighbors that has been given. But the theme is strongly connected to "the beginning". My question is which beginning is this referring to. Some may say, the beginning points to when John first began to minister to the people he is writing to now. And I can go along with that. But, let's take it a little deeper. We see the phrase "no new commandment" and "old commandment". The word "old" when you look it up in the Greek is the word "palaios" which means ancient and worn at the worst level by use. It points to something very old. You might be saying well yes, the commandment of love has been there since the old testament. But the context of the scripture is that you had the ancient commandment from the beginning of its inception. Not only have you had this from the beginning, you also heard it from the beginning. If you look at this from that view, it changes things considerably.

We have a testimony, a record, a witness in us that even though at times has been hidden, things come along our path that begins to resonate with what is already in us. In the first chapter of the gospel of John, we are reminded that Christ is the light that lights every man that comes into the world. In other words, there is a part of Christ that is placed on or in every human being that comes in the world and that light is waiting to be ignited and breathed upon for its increase. That is why the gospel of Christ is so important because we can't believe, unless we hear. And we can't hear, unless someone preaches. And that person can't preach unless they are sent. Why are they sent from God the Father? Because the Father knows by his design that there is something in you waiting to be lit by that gospel word of life. This word begins to resonate with the light that is deep down in our being. This is where deep calls to deep to come forth. This is an example of the birthing of new life in us through our faith in the gospel of Christ. But it works the same way with walking out our realized destiny, which is the finishing of our salvation.

Pieces of our destiny is in us as a record that we had and heard from the beginning. And God not only sends people with the gospel of the kingdom to ignite salvation but he will use people and events to help stir up the destiny within to rise to the surface. Sometimes there is an intuition of what is in you. At other times, you see something on television or read something in a book or hear a saying and something in you just begins to take you to something familiar. This should be when we begin to pay attention and take note that God is using something or someone to lead us back to him and his purposes for our lives. As we take note, the next step is to come in agreement with that which we had and heard from the beginning. In doing this, we began and continue to be witnesses to the world as we proclaim and live out the testimony from the beginning which is Christ Jesus. He is the beginning and the end. Let's come into agreement with Him.

Jesus is the Pattern We Follow

Jesus Christ is the beginning. Jesus Christ is the firstborn of creation. Jesus Christ is the begotten Son of God. And it pleased the Father to destined us before the foundation of the world to be conformed to the image and pattern of his Son Jesus Christ. Why? This was done so Christ may be the firstborn among many brothers and sisters. However, you slice it, Jesus is the first of all things and our goal is to walk even as he walked. We are to follow his lead so that we can be mature sons walking in the full stature of Christ. The Father made a mold and he wants to use that mold to shape and mold us into the image of his Son. Jesus Christ is the pattern Son.

The plan of redemption was established in the beginning before the foundation of the world. The lamb was slain before the foundation of the world. The notion that the Son would have to manifest in the world in a body was well established before the foundation of the world. Hebrews 10:5 shares that Christ knew that the blood of bulls and goats would not suffice as an eternal solution for taking aways the sins of mankind. So the Father in conjunction with the Son's agreement to the redemption plan prepared Christ a body to be manifested in the earth in its given time. And in the realm of eternity, where the end is declared from the beginning, the Father considers the slaying of the Lamb already done. For this purpose, the Son fully seeing what the Father wanted to accomplish chose to come forth in the fullness of the Father and agree to be the sacrifice. He saw and said, "Yes Father, send me" and a body was prepared for the savior of the world to fulfill the book and scroll that was written of him. Of course, the Son has a scroll as it is stated in Hebrews 10:7 that "Lo, I come in the volume of the book it is written of me to do thy will, O God". He is the first and the pattern in all things and we have to follow the same process as he did.

25

We have discussed before how Jeremiah and Paul how God foreknew them before they were formed in their mother's womb and called them to a certain destiny. We see how Christ had a certain destiny that was contained in books and scrolls in heaven to fulfill. So as the pattern Son is, so are we where we have to walk the same pathway for he is the way, the truth, and the life. So Christ overcame the world and so should we. Christ was crucified and that is why we must be crucified with him and be made conformable to his death. Christ rose again and we are called to be partakers of that same resurrection power. Christ ascended to the right hand of the Father and we are called to set out affections on things above as we come into realization that we sit together with him in heavenly places. He is the pattern and the way and it is by looking at Christ the author and finisher of our faith and through Christ that we will align and fulfill this testimony within us.

Isaiah As An Example

Isaiah 6 (KJV)
8 Also I heard the voice of the Lord, saying, Whom shall I send, and who will go for us? Then said I, Here am I; send me.

I want to refer to the above scripture and use Isaiah as an example. In this context, Isaiah in the year King Uzziah died, had an encounter with the realm of heaven and eternity. He saw the throne room with the Most High high and lifted up and the temple was filled with the glory of God. He saw the particular angels and in that realm, had a revelation that he was a man of unclean lips. At that moment, a seraphim grabs a coal and places the coal on his lips and proclaims to him that his iniquity and sins were purged. This is highly significant because from the placing of the coal, a shift happened. Isaiah realizes that he is a man of unclean lips because in the higher realms you can see things clearly and he realizes that what he has spoken and what was in him did not fully line up with the witness and testimony of heaven.

He acknowledges this and the Most High rectifies the situation causing his sin to be purged and his iniquity which is that within you that causes you to miss the mark to be taken away. This is very similar to what the blood of the lamb and the word of his testimony does. The blood of the Lamb purges your sin and takes away iniquity so that you can now walk in the new creation you were called to be from eternity.

This leads to verse 8 above. After the touch from the Most High, it has been revealed to me that a shift happens to cause him to remember and hear a conversation that he had in the realm of eternity before he came into the world. Remember God does not live in the realm of time but only manifests in the realm of time. So when Isaiah is lifted into that realm, the beginning and ending live there at the same time and he begins to hear the witness connected to heaven and his spirit begins to replay what he had and heard from the beginning. And it said, "Whom will I send and who will go for us?" And Isaiah said in return now aligning to the testimony connected to his spirit and echoing its intent, says "Here am I, send me". And then the rest is released to him to go and say. This is probably the first encounter with the Most High like this and the first where he realizes that he was called to be a prophet to the nation of Israel before the foundation of the world.

It was revealed that Isaiah in the Father and in the realm of eternity had a conversation before the host of heaven and us as well saying who will go for this particular reason. The reason why we know it was not just the Most High present during the conversation is because it says "go for us". We were all there seeing parts of the plan of the Most High on the earth and he was saying who will go for this and who will go for that. And when certain assignments were discussed and who would go, we came forward and said "Here am I, send me". We asked for him to prepare a body for us so we can do his bidding and pleasure on the earth. This will be discussed in future chapters but when we came into the earth there was a dynamic that hid our calling from us and we all have to come to a place like Isaiah where it is realized once again. Just like Isaiah, who came out of eternity with an expectation and later came to know that expectation, we must walk in that same process to become aware of the same expectation that God has for our lives.

Hints In Book of Job

Job 38 (KJV)

1 Then the Lord answered Job out of the whirlwind, and said,

*2 Who is this that darkeneth counsel by **words without knowledge?***

*3 Gird up now thy loins **like a man**; for I will demand of thee, and answer thou me.*

*4 **Where wast thou when I laid the foundations of the earth? declare, if thou hast understanding.***

5 Who hath laid the measures thereof, if thou knowest? or who hath stretched the line upon it?

6 Whereupon are the foundations thereof fastened? or who laid the corner stone thereof;

*7 When the **morning stars sang together**, and **all the sons of God shouted for joy?***

Jesus is truly the pattern son and he is before us all. He is the first in everything. With this in mind, let's look at the book of Job. I like the book of Job because if you are looking with the heart of the Spirit of God, there are some nuggets in the book of Job. As most of us know, Job was a righteous man before God and through a conversation between the enemy and God, Job was chosen to be tried by the enemy with the restriction that he could not be killed. It was rough. He lost his kids and all that he owned. His wife and friends wanted him to curse God and die. But through his steadfastness in his trust in God, he endured and ended up with double blessing after this trial of his faith. You might be wondering what does the story of Job has to do with Jesus, eternity, and us before we came on the earth. Let's take a deeper look.

Most of the book of Job up to the 38th chapter was pretty intense even where Job eventually cursed the day he was born. This declaration got God's attention and he began to have a conversation with Job in chapter 38. God starts off with saying who has darkened your mind that caused you to use words without knowledge and wisdom. God continues to tell Job to gird up himself like a man. I don't believe this is like we see today where you tell someone to man up in a macho way. But this was the Most High saying remember who you are. You are a man made in the image and likeness of God and you are here for a purpose. As the chapter goes along, a lot of theologians and scholars believe that God begins to take a sarcastic and haughty tone with Job. But that is not the case because our God is telling him to gird himself and his intention is to encourage him and bring forth understanding to him.

God begins to remind Job who he is and that he is more than just a man in a temporal earth. He proceeds to ask Job a question. Where were you when I laid the foundations of earth? Then he says declare it if you have understanding. But he knows Job can't declare it because he starts off to say Job did not have understanding. God as the chapter goes along began to highlight aspects of creation to hint that Job was there when some of these things were happening but he does not have the full wisdom and understanding of it. He is not taunting Job to say look how big I am and look how little you are. No, he is reminding Job of himself before he was on earth.

Verse 7 takes it to another level. It mentions when the morning stars sang together and the sons of God shouted for joy at the sight of creation. Who do you think these morning stars and sons of God are? Jesus is the pattern and the first. He is the eldest brother. We refer to Jesus as the morning star and we also refer to him as the Son of God. So if we are like him on some level, then we were also morning stars and sons of God. We sang and shouted with praise because we had assignments and destiny to fulfill in this creation called earth. Sonship is a big component of the gospel and redemption story of Christ from an eternal perspective. I hope this excites you as much as it does me. We were there during creation viewing it as it happened. I also believe we played some part of it. Why do I say that? It is part of how God operates. God gets his firstborn Son in on the creation and the firstborn Son gets his younger siblings to help on some level. When Christ returns for his glorious and overcoming church to establish the kingdom of God and create a new heaven and earth, he will not do it alone. We, as mature sons, will have a heavier role in this new creation because all of creation groans for the manifestation of the sons of God. We are the "sons of God" mentioned in verse 7 but right now it does not yet appear what and who we are. But one day, the full manifestation will be revealed.

Job 38 (KJV)

21 Knowest thou it, because thou wast then born? or because the number of thy days is great?

Job 38 (TLB)

19 Where does the light come from, and how do you get there? Or tell me about the darkness. Where does it come from? 20 Can you find its boundaries, or go to its source? ***21 But of course you know all this! For you were born before it was all created, and you are so very experienced!***

Later there is a key verse I want to point to you which is verse 21 listed above. From a KJV translation, this passage is posed as a question almost like God is being demeaning, snobbish, or sarcastic. That is not his character and his intention at the moment is to build Job up. God's character is truth and love. A lot of other Hebrew scholars believe that the translation that gets closer to the intention of the verse is the Living Bible (TLB). This version does not pose a question but indeed makes a declaration that of course you know all this deep within you because you were born before it all was created and you are very old and experienced. Wow, how this changes the perspective to show that we were created before in eternity and were sent into earth. We were not only witnesses to aspects of creation but we understood it was made for us and we agreed to come out of the realms of eternity with a testimony scroll to fulfill the destiny of our Father.

Prayer

Heavenly Father who reigns in eternity, I pray that you grant all who read this book to become aware of the expectation you have for their lives. I pray that a yearning rises in them to crave to please you. I pray that a conversion happens in their inner man to cause them to encounter the Lord to reveal the hope of his calling in their hearts and grace them to walk in the fullness of that calling. In Jesus name. Amen.

Chapter 3 : IT IS IN YOU

* * *

The ecstatic level in me is so high right now thinking about how there is a God that is above all who is filled with wisdom and power. He is the master builder and implementer of his will in the heavens and earth. Who is like him? The answer is simply no one. His mind is full of us with his aligning purposes and expected ends he has in store for us. He has even written books and scrolls in the halls of heaven with every strategic detail mapped out. These scrolls with our name on them containing outlining assignments of the Father were released in the "was" before the beginning of the earth. We witnessed this and the glory of the Father. Some may wonder if these records and testimonies of the will of God live in the realms above the earth, then how if we were sent to earth, supposed to be accountable to fulfilling what is on the scroll? The answer to this is that we came out of eternity with a testimony and destiny and it lives in us. It is in you and I. Then the next inquiry might be if it is in us, then why don't we remember our time before and/or our testimony of before? Why can't we just read the testimony scroll of destiny with ease since it is right there within us? My aim is to answer these types of questions in this chapter as we first start with the beginning of Adam.

Before the Fall

In the beginning, God created the heavens and the earth. And they (the Godhead) said, "Let us make man in our image and likeness". And God began to proceed and make Adam out of the dust of ground and breathed into his nostrils a piece of himself and spirit (breath) and Adam became a living soul. And out of Adam, came Eve and they both were living souls unto God. They were in a sense, naked but not ashamed because they were covered with the glory of God. The reason the glory and light of God was covering them was because they were spirit beings hosting within them their soul and body. The spirit body was bigger than the physical body and they lived by their spirit man. They communed with God by their spirit man.

Also, because they communed with God by their spirit, their purpose and the sound of their scroll was always before them. They knew their assignment. They knew their domain and calling. They knew that they were to be fruitful and multiply and have dominion over the birds, cattle, and fish. They were also placed in a garden in Eden and commanded to protect, keep, and dress the garden. There were four rivers connected to this garden and rivers of living water flowed through this garden. God Almighty talked with them in the cool of the day spirit to spirit. There were even certain restrictions like don't eat from a certain tree. Adam knew his place as a visionary carrying a mandate and that with Eve's mandate as a helper, they together in unity and harmony will fulfill the scroll of destiny assigned to them by their heavenly father.

Things were great. They were enjoying fellowship with God. Eden was beautiful, restful, and bountiful. They knew who they were and why they were there. The expectations and restrictions of God were clear to them because they lived by their spirit and were not hindered by a fallen world or an enemy. Adam and Eve were good because they were filled with the nature of God but they were not mature and perfected yet. The only way to make sure something is mature is through proving and testing. That is surely what that old serpent did in the garden. We know how the story in Genesis goes, the enemy got Adam and Eve to take their eyes off of their scroll of destiny and the commandments of God. In turn, they believed the lie of the enemy and began to desire that which was not ordained from the Lord and misaligned themselves from their destiny. This resulted in a changed nature which we refer to as "The Fall".

After the Fall

"The Fall" changed everything. Not only did it change the nature of Adam and Eve but it changed their position from a spiritual level and also their plain of existence. From this plain of existence, their mode of communication changed. No longer were they living in a realm of unlimited blessings but now succumbed to a life full of curses. There was a shift from a position of rest to a posture and lifestyle of hard work, sweat, and pain. The structure of their DNA was altered in many ways and the impact of the fall not only impacted them but also the offspring that would one day be on earth. These changes of them and this world would be felt on some level to all who were born in this physical plan for generations .

Before it was stated that Adam and Eve before the fall, were spirit beings filled with glory and light hosting the soul and body within them. But the fall changed out of that. When the forbidden fruit was eaten, they knew right away because the glory essence of their spirit imploded into them. That which was outside became and inside and that which was inside became outside. Their physical body which was naked was inside. They were not ashamed because they were covered by their spiritual body which was full of glory and light. But when the spiritual body imploded inside, the physical body came to the forefront. Before it was being hosted by the spirit man so it did not need any skin. Adam and Eve knew right away they needed to be covered and try to do it themselves. This is why God had to give us coats of skin because we did not possess skin like that at first. Now mankind was subjected to life by the dictates and desires of their body because the lust of the flesh, the lust of the eye , and pride of life was awakened in the physical body. The physical body's sin nature awakened enough to grow the physical body enough to encase the spirit and soul so it can take the lead.

The spirit man now was being hosted by the physical body and now shrunken and smothered within. Therefore the glory and light in a sense died out and went deep inside. Also, everything connected to Eden with the presence of God, its garden and rivers also was pushed deep inside as well. As the physical heart has 4 chambers and flows of blood, also the heart of man has the 4 rivers of Eden within him. Instead of soul being a living soul that was led by the source of the spirit man. The soul now was dead because now the life giving source of the spirit man was hidden and the physical flesh body now is in the driver seat. This new setup impacted mankind's awareness of God and the plane on which he can live.

No longer could we enjoy the fullness of the garden of Eden in all its glory. No longer could we have the same face to face interaction with God like Adam and Eve once relished and appreciated. The clarity of our original destiny and what was commanded of us was made opaque. Adam and Eve were driven from the perspective of knowing Earth through the eyes of the spirit and heart to knowing the world through the eyes and other senses of the physical body. They were driven out of the garden of rest to a fallen and cursed creation. Due to lack of the access and supply of the fullness of God, they had to trust in the ability of their brain, emotions and reasoning of their soul and body. For the true connection to the glory of God and his plans of destiny for mankind was broken and hidden. There was definitely a need for the soul of man to be revived so that the spirit of man can be one with the Spirit of God once again. Glory be to God that "the fall" did not catch the foreknowing God. The Lamb of God was slain before the foundation of the world to reconcile mankind back to God through his Son.

From Heaven to Earth

Some background information concerning Adam and Eve before and after the fall had to be covered as a foundation. In the mind of God, we were created as spiritual beings before we came to earth. There was an expectation for each one of our lives expressed through the Word (Jesus Christ) on tablets, scrolls, and books in eternity. We remain in the Father awaiting our destined time to be birthed in the earth through a womb. We have a testimony and eyewitness account of God's destiny for our lives from that realm of eternity and we are excitedly awaiting to walk in it. But due to the fall and the fact that now the spirit and heart of man that would be the housing of the scroll of God is now hidden deep in man. Let's look closer at the process that happens at conception.

God has the power of life. No life is by accident in the eyes of God. Everyone was born for a specific time and purpose. It is not by the will of man that someone else is born. This is why you might have a couple trying for a baby for years and don't get one till 5 years down the line because there is a timing in play. Just because procreation activities does not always mean a child will be conceived. On the other side of the coin, sometimes unfortunate things like rape and incest occurs and children are born out of these scenarios. In God's infinite wisdom, he has chosen these windows of opportunities to bring spirit beings out of heaven into earth. Some people's mind is to end all pregnancies from this type of situation but these are not accidents in God's eyes. Not that God ordained the action but he used that window to bring destiny into the world. It surprises me as some of the greats throughout time who were the products of things like rape and incest, but God did something amazing through their lives to impact the world. Once again, our heavenly Father thoughts are not our thoughts and his ways are not our ways.

When there are procreation activities going on in the world, and the Father has ordained purpose, a spirit being with a testimony scroll of destiny is sent from eternity to the earth. This being is ready to make its earth debut inside of that woman to enter in when that sperm meets with the egg. Did you know in this decade of the 2010s that scientists have been able to capture through some technological device what happens at conception. What has been explained is that when the sperm collides into the egg, a spark and flash of light happens. From revelation of the Holy Spirit, I know that this spark of light is the entrance of the spirit-soul being introduced into this physical plane. A being of light lit by Christ himself containing the scroll record of destiny with it. The bible also confirms this in the first chapter of the gospel of John. In verse 9, it states that Christ is the true light that lights every man that comes into the world. Every spirit being from on high came with the light of Christ and breath of God. This light was a way ordained for each life that came with every inserted soul. Please know that you came out of eternity as a child of the Father with a testimony scroll of destiny and light into your mother's womb. You are the planting of the Lord in the earth.

The Scroll Is Deep In You

Your spirit man along with your testimony scroll bursting with light arrives and becomes one with the first cell that is created by the sperm egg combination. That scroll is there from the onset. Your spirit man is filled with the spiritual DNA of the Father embedded with light and your destiny image of what you are supposed to form to be. From there, cells begin to multiply. But the original cell goes into the middle of your being and forms the heart. It is very interesting that the heart is the first formed organ. With the spiritual destiny and DNA linked to the first cell, the heart began to form and encase that original cell. In a sense, as the heart, other organs, and body parts are formed, this record from heaven is smothered within. Due to the implosion and fall of man, we are made in the image of the fallen Adam which our physical body now hosts our spirit man. That spirit man with the testimony is hidden deep and wrapped around with our body.

This is half the reason why we don't remember why we came and who we were before our existence on earth. The spirit is smothered by the physical body. I want to note that the spirit and testimony scroll (spiritual DNA) is not just sitting there doing nothing. It is vibrating at a spiritual level and frequency creating a song to be heard. Oh I love this because through scriptures we know that there is a song of Moses and a song of Hannah. But in the book of Revelation, it also dictates that the redeemed of the Lord will sing a song that only they and the Most High knows. That is the goal here to be able with our lives to sing that song of being redeemed and overcomers by reaching the finish line. One of the problems is that the song of the Lord , if I can say, is being stifled and padded by being encased in the flesh of our heart.

The second issue is this. Because we are spirit, soul, and body. As the spirit is vibrating out a song, our soul, and physical body is as well. The soul is like a middle man who is going to harmonize with either the physical body or the spirit man depending who is singing the loudest. In the perfect world, the spirit, soul, and body would all be singing the same song with the spirit man singing the lead and melody where the soul and body align in harmony according to the melody of the spirit man. What a great picture of unity of our triune being. But because of the fall this is not the case. In most cases, the physical DNA of the body is (vibrating) singing a song much louder than that of the spirit man because its song is insulated in the heart of the fallen man. There is dissonance in the singing group and two parties want to take the lead. The spirit is at enmity with the flesh and vice versa. The chaos that lives in man due to the fall of Adam and Eve.

Scientists also have confirmed that the physical DNA of man not only contains genetic code on how your physical body is supposed to form into. But it also vibrates at a certain frequency and sings a song as well. All of the songs of our DNA are unique due to the combination of our parents' chromosomes. We all have 46 chromosomes with 23 from each parent. As our spiritual DNA wrapped in our heart contains a testimony of genetic

CHAPTER 3 : IT IS IN YOU

code and events from heaven, our physical DNA contains a testimony of genetic code and events on earth all the way back to Adam and the fall. Our spiritual testimony goes back to the source of our destiny and being in eternity. The physical testimony of our DNA contains a record of all habits, curses, and traits of your bloodline on both sides of your family starting from when Adam was separated from Eden. And this song of generations of voices is singing loud from your physical being louder than the song of your spirit man. Your spirit man is singing, you are a child of the King. But your physical self is vibrating at a certain frequency, a song that you are defeated and cursed and just a product of your physical ancestors carrying and reaping what they have sown into you.

So the combination of the testimony scroll of heaven being padded in our heart and also competing with the testimony of our flesh, it makes it very hard to hear the testimony song of our spirit man. That is why we need the spirit man to be revived and born again through the sacrifice of Jesus Christ, the Lamb of God. Oh the power of the blood of Jesus that is worthy to blot out the records and testimonies against us that speak death and judgment to us. Hebrews 12 lets us know that the blood of Jesus speaks with a testimony that is greater and better than the testimony of Abel. The testimony of Jesus is that which was spoken to us in the beginning. The testimony Abel holds is the testimony of the DNA of fallen Adam that once was a living soul that is now dead. And this was one of Adam's righteous sons. The blood of Jesus holds the testimony of a quickening spirit which can make us alive again unto the hope of glory. We need the combination of the blood of Jesus and the Word of our testimony scroll. This is how we overcome the enemy in this world. Know that the testimony scroll of destiny is deep within you, hidden and muffled. Believe the gospel of Christ and receive the blood of his sacrifice and then will birth your spirit man again so that you can begin to hear the song of testimony of eternity and destiny. And through the beginning of your journey began to change the song of your soul and even your mortal body to align with the scrolls of destiny in you.

Cloning and Abortion

At the point the sperm hits an egg and conception happens, life begins there. This a spiritual being holding a destiny within a womb. Some believe ignorantly are looking at life starting once a baby is delivered from the womb into the world. This is them looking at things from a skewed physical perspective. But since we are spirit before physical, the spiritual perspective alludes to that we are alive at the moment of conception. That fetus is an individual even at that point in the world within a womb on an assignment from God Almighty.

This is why the action of abortion stabs at the heart of the Father. When a baby is aborted , a destiny is aborted in the world. I don't say this to condemn those who have in ignorance or knowingly done this. But know his forgiveness and healing is available for you right now. Just turn to him and let the blood and love of Jesus cleanse and cover you. The good news is that those babies' spirits are received back unto God in a special place in heaven. But that record of the blood in the earth is crying out up to the throne of heaven. When we see governments and legislation as proponent for abortion, there is a diabolical plan of the enemy behind it. He wants to cut off as many destinies as he can so he will not be defeated. It is his way to kill, steal, and destroy. The babies in the womb are very dear to the Father because it is his intent to mature these spirits from him to mature sons of the Kingdom.

Now on to cloning. God holds the power of life to create a human being that will be a triune being of spirit, soul, and body. So in reality, the origin of that birth is from heaven and comes along with a destiny. But when scientists are in a place where they are trying to mimic God and begin to manipulate DNA and begin to clone individuals, what is the source of this creation? It does not originate from heaven. I believe that the inner self of a clone is not complete because it lacks the special ingredient that only God from above

40

can give. And if the source is not God, then what spirit is providing that source? I believe this is another demonic agenda where the enemy is trying to counterfeit the workings of God and build up his own family. Notice that in Genesis 3, it says that the seed of the woman will bruise the head of the seed of the serpent. There is spiritual seed and physical seed. It is recorded where the enemy tried to pervert the physical seed of man. Is it possible that cloning is the enemy agenda to pervert the spiritual seed of man? In any case, the only true testimony is the testimony of God from the beginning. Any other agenda that goes against that is out of order. Abortions cancels out testimonies of destiny and cloning tries to circumvent testimonies of destiny. In these, God is not pleased.

Tethered

I want to convey another piece of information received by the spirit of revelation and wisdom. During the fall, mankind's fallen nature and physical body was tethered to this natural world. The result of this is that the source of strength and guidance from heaven took a back seat to the guidance of the god of this world. Its knowledge and influence only could go as high as the atmosphere because that is the high point of the earth realm. The god of this world (Satan) is known as the prince of the power of the air. So if we are not led by the spirit of God in our spirit man, then we are led by the spirit of disobedience that reigns on this earth. In the fallen state, we are connected to the influence of the enemy and also referred to in that state as children of the devil.

The highest influence is that of the stars, the planets, the moon, and sun. What is interesting is that this is what the zodiac is based off of. There are sun signs based on a position of the constellation of stars at a given time. If you go deeper you realize that there are moon signs and other signs based on the planets that are looking at star alignment. The twelve constellations (another story another time) are actually creations of the Most High that tells the gospel of the Kingdom but the enemy has distorted things and used it for other purposes. Also, even the other planets in what we call our solar system are actually disobedient wandering stars that God has held in position for judgment until the end times. People are worshipping these planets and a lot of the pagan gods are aligned to these planets. People are very much into astrology and the zodiac of the stars. But if we look in God's word, we see that God is against the consulting of astrology with its omens and horoscopes.

The problem is if we are living by the dictates of our physical body that is tethered to this earth, then our flesh will align to the plan and in a sense "the scroll" of the enemy. That is why some people are saying I am a Scorpio. Some are claiming I am a Libra. I am a Taurus. When we do this, we are only saying that I come in agreement with who the prince of the power of the air says I am. We are saying with this proclamation that I am under the control of the stars and not God. I am not saying that you are not going to read a book about Aries and you are not going to see some truths about that person you know who was born in a certain time range. The enemy has been around for centuries and have gathered some information here and there based on patterns. But what I want to emphasize is that if you are able to read one of those books and it is able to predict who you are and all your characteristic traits, then that is proof you are not under the influence of the spirit of God. Why send Jesus the Messiah if all we had to do is look to the stars and know who we are supposed to be. There is a higher wisdom and leading that God wants us to seek. He does not want us to be conformed to the world and its influence but be renewed by Christ to prove what is the perfect will of God.

Most things that are displayed in this physical world are there to show a pattern that was established in heaven. It is used to be clues or an analogy to seek the higher things of God. So I don't find it a strange coincidence that there are 12 star constellations and also 12 tribes of Israel. God wanted to pick a bloodline to be a symbol and pattern of what he already ordained in heaven. He already ordained a family in heaven that he calls his own. Ephesians 3:15 lets us know that the whole family in heaven and earth is named and filled with the DNA of God. In other words, when we were in the Father we were part of a huge family of God. And using God's pattern, we were separated into 12 tribes of family. Each tribe of heaven represents certain giftings, callings, and destinies. So in God, you are not part of a zodiac sign but born again to a tribe in the family of God.

I believe that there are certain promises to the physical bloodline of Jacob (Israel) but with Christ we are now a new creation and behold all things are made new. He has caused the Jew and the Gentile to be made one new man. And spiritually, to the man or woman who is circumcised in their heart, they are Jew inwardly by the spirit. God no longer identifies you fully by your physical DNA but by your spiritual DNA. That is why in Revelation 14, there is a company of the 144,000 who have the Father's name written in their foreheads as sons of the Most High. And then it further goes on to name the different tribes of spiritual Israel. Born again by God in spirit causes you to know that you are named in the family of the Father that is heaven and earth. You are on earth but you contain a testimony of heaven in you that has your true name from the Father and destiny. The key is to untethered yourself from this world and its influences through Christ and be born again by the Spirit of God to awaken your spirit man to be tethered to a higher influence which is the throng of God. As a child of God, no longer identify with a zodiac sign, but with the sign of Jesus that aligns you with the family of the Father.

Hidden In Your Heart

Luke 17:21 lets us know that we can search all over and try to find the kingdom of God, but the kingdom of God is within you. The word kingdom broken down is king's domain. A domain is a territory, realm, or particular space that you have rulership over. The Lord is the King of kings. Who are those kings that he is King over? We are!!! This is the center of the gospel of the kingdom. That there is a territory that we are called to possess and be joint heirs with Jesus. I am telling you today that the beginning of walking in that kingdom of Christ is locating the testimony scroll of destiny that is hidden in your heart. That testimony scroll outlines your part and your piece of the kingdom that God ordained for you to walk in the earth. There is a call that you are separated to that only you can possess and rule over. It is your domain that under the guiding and power of Christ, you can be overcomers over this domain. There is a charge in Matthew 6:33 that admonishes us to seek you first the kingdom of God.

The kingdom of God with the King of kings and its instructions are hidden within you. The testimony that you came out of heaven with is hidden and smothered within your heart trying to get a song to you. It is under the ruins of the fall of man and another structure has been built over it trying to out sing the song that you carry from heaven. It is all concealed within you. The quest that the Most High has charged you with to become born again by the sacrifice of the blood of Jesus and the Holy Spirit and begin in the adventure of finding that hidden treasure in earthen vessels. That testimony scroll of destiny is deep within you covered in darkness and you only can fully find it and align with it through Christ Jesus. This scroll must be found and then unraveled for the sake of the King of kings.

Prayer

Heavenly Father, Abba, I pray according to Colossians 1:9-12 that the reader of this book be filled with the knowledge of Your will and the destiny for their lives. That in all wisdom and spiritual understanding, they may continue to have a walk worthy of You that aligns with their scroll of destiny within them. Father I pray that they be fully pleasing to You, by being fruitful in every good work. Father, increase not just in their purpose but also the knowledge of you. Bless them to be strengthened with all might to fight this war against the enemy according to Your glorious power. Fill them with all patience and long-suffering with joy as they seek you and their destiny. Father, qualify them to be filled with light so they can find that which is deep and obscure in them. Reveal all to them in the glory of your name. Amen.

Chapter 4 : FIND & UNRAVEL

***

That which the Most High God has placed in mankind is awesome and wonderful. Words can't express his love for and faith in mankind. His thoughts towards us are filled with peace and expectation for us to come in the knowledge of his will for our lives so we allow his purposes to unfold in the earth. There is a scripture in Proverbs 25:2 that I love to meditate upon and even quote from time to time. It relates that it is the glory of the Lord to conceal a matter. When we talk about the testimony scrolls in us and even the way to communion with the Father and the Lord Jesus. It is guarded. With Adam and Eve, when they were expelled from the garden, the way to the garden was guarded by the cherubim with the flaming swords. That place of communion and life in the Lord lives in us . Mankind was not kicked out for it to be that way forever but it was his plan for us to return and exceed that moment.

As I am writing this, I am reminded that it was not just Adam and Eve who were expelled, but that old serpent as well. The enemy has been kicked out never to return. But there is a way that is hidden and guarded that we must long for and look for. It is concealed by the Lord but he wants us to find it. The way is guarded and we have to go through the flaming sword to get back to it. The sword is the Word of God and we need to be changed and penetrated by the fire of God. This way is narrow and few find it. For many are called but few are chosen. The chosen are those who heed the call to press and seek with all diligence to please the Lord. The root of the word "chosen" is the same as "elect" and "holy". It is the set apart ones who will find the way and be overcomers in the quest that is set before them.

What is inside us is referred to as treasures in earthen vessels. It is precious and God has allowed certain things to be concealed so that the pearls won't be trampled by the swine. So the babes won't squander and dismantle that which is valuable. Also, the way has been concealed so the enemy does not have the inside track and you are not wide open and vulnerable to his attacks. It is in the wisdom and glory of the Lord that your scroll is hidden deep with you and protected. It is marked top secret and for your eyes and those eyes who he has deemed worthy to know his secrets. Gather all the tools you need and pack up your backpack for the greatest scavenger hunt you will embark on; the quest for the secret files with your name on it.

An Agricultural Perspective

I don't claim to know much about agriculture sciences at all. For a year, I had an opportunity to work for a global agricultural company. It was quite the learning experience. I was amazed at the time, science, technology and effort that was appropriated to the agricultural mission of this company. I was there to be a coach to help teams collaborate together efficiently and uphold certain industry standards when it came to the information technology arena. Before this I looked at farming as simply planting a seed, watering it, and harvesting the crop to distribute to the needed parties. But the eye opener was the strategic workings that happened even before a seed was planted in the ground for market purposes.

There was genetic engineering and experimentation. The flow of crop science went deeper than I could ever imagine. Without going into too much detail, I work with a few teams where their goal was to create software that could use GPS coordinates to view a field and separate that field into min plots of land. From there, then map out the min plots and assign which type of seed will be in each mini section. Then, compile all that information with the seeds and coordinates and encode in a computer storage center that can be attached to an automated seed planter machine that can then plant seeds in given areas according to the sequence that was already pre-programmed. It was a well thought out scheme of strategic planning, implementation, and automation. I was open-mouthed, tongue hanging to the floor amazed at the presentation of this.

While writing this book, I thought of this example because the testimony scrolls of God are hidden in our heart. And our heart is a garden that was established by the Lord within us that is waiting for the right plan and seed to be planted. Remember the garden of Eden was imploded into man from the fall. I begin to liken the crop scientist unto God Almighty who has mapped our lives into different mini sections and has embedded the data into our spiritual DNA from heaven and placed it in our heart. The issue is that it is hidden, guarded, and even locked up in our heart. We need to be guided and led by the Holy Spirit to find the guarded and locked place and use Christ Jesus who is the key to unlock the storehouse of seeds and instructions.

After finding and opening the storehouse that is within your heart, then regular agriculture methods apply. It is more than just knowing what the call and destiny is, you have to get the seed in the right place so it can be sowed, watered, harvested, and out to market. This reminds me of when I was a kid and I used to look at the GI Joe cartoons. At the end there was a slogan that always stuck with me. That slogan was "Knowing is half the battle". Even as a kid it made me ponder and I found it profound. But this applies here spiritually, even when you become in the know, there is an application and process that must be stepped through to win this war that we are in against

48

the enemy. His goal is to stop you from being overcomers and our goal should be to fulfill the destiny outlined from eternity on the scrolls within our heart. When we are not using the right heavenly template or blueprint, the wrong seeds are planted and tares sprout up instead of wheat. We need to acknowledge the Lord in all our ways and utilize the tools he has provided, so he can direct our paths.

Start by Asking

Matthew 7 (KJV)
7 Ask, and it shall be given you; seek, and ye shall find; knock, and it shall be opened unto you:
8 For every one that asketh receiveth; and he that seeketh findeth; and to him that knocketh it shall be opened.

Now that the foundation has been laid that we have a scroll of destiny with us, the question might be now how do we begin the process of finding this scroll and its contents. In simplicity, the answer is ask for it and it will be given. Jesus Christ has given us the guarantee that everyone who asks, will receive. We have to have faith that whatever we have petitioned the Lord in, that he will definitely give to us. The thing is that sometimes our heavenly Father enjoys a good game of hide and seek. I believe he does things like this to see if you really want it or not. Sometimes we live in a time where people are looking for gifts and hand me outs. They are searching for the quick and easy hook up. But God is looking to see if you are longing for the things of God with all your heart, mind, soul, and strength.

His method is like a kid who asks for a present, but when it is time to receive the present, the present has been wrapped up , placed in a locked box positioned in a hidden place. And the goal is for this kid to search this whole field or place for the hidden prize (pearl) that is indeed the score of a lifetime. It is almost like those movies where people are looking for the treasure map that eventually will take them to the treasure. The scroll is the treasure map. The destiny is where the scroll points you to. And it will be an adventure just to get your hands on the treasure map. But the price of admission to this journey is the asking from you. It is yours for the asking, but you have to seek for it.

Seek & Find

If God wants us to walk in our destiny so badly, then why does it seem like it is so hidden and it is a hassle to know it? The reason as it was revealed to me is because we have an enemy. If this scroll was just out in the open where anyone can get to it, the enemy no doubt would try to destroy it before you can get your hands on it. Also, sometimes parts of the scroll will not all come to you at once because God is a line upon line and precept upon precept God . So the scroll is revealed in pieces and in seasons. If it all came at once and the devil knew the fullness of it, he could then counter right away and the battle would be over, finished, done. But our God has infinite wisdom and as the saying goes, "Father knows best". So we must press pass just asking and go to the next step of seeking so we can find.

Ephesians 1 (KJV)
17 That the God of our Lord Jesus Christ, the Father of glory, may give unto you **the spirit of wisdom and revelation** *in the* **knowledge of him** *(relationship):* *18* **The eyes of your understanding** *being enlightened; that ye may know what is the* **hope of his calling** *(revelation), and what the riches of the glory of his inheritance in the saints,*

The above scripture is probably my favorite. But excuse me if I say that about some others as well. (laugh) But seriously, I meditate on this scripture many times a day. I believe it is a key to walking in much spiritual revelation and understanding. So if you want to know what you should ask in the first step, you can start off with this scripture. This is important because to seek for something you have to be able to see. Did you ever notice that the word "see" is part of the word "seek"? The prayer of these verses is asking for the spirit of wisdom and revelation to endow us so our inward eyes can see. Which eyes? The eyes of our understanding which are the eyes of our heart. Remember, the scroll is hidden in the darkness in our hearts so we need the eyes of our heart to be filled with light to commence this search.

Once the eyes of our heart are filled with light, then we can have understanding. There are many things we can want understanding in but it is clear that the spirit of wisdom and revelation will reveal a certain type of understanding. The verse continues to say that we will be enlightened to know what is the hope of his calling. This speaks of God's destiny for our life. Hope speaks to that there was an expectation that was placed in us. This hope and expectation is on the scroll within us. We now need the spiritual eyes that were imploded within mankind during the fall of man to be awakened and come into focus. The activation of the eyes of our heart by the spirit of wisdom and revelation will aid us considerably in the quest to see the testimony scroll and its contents. We must pursue to see that which is spiritual with spiritual eyes so that we can find it.

Knock Hard

There is an asking and then a seeking but when you find it, you will see that it is a door that you must go through as well. The beauty is that all things are by Christ Jesus. He is the door and the key to the door. He is also the only one who can open the door. In review, you ask for the Holy Spirit who will lead you to Christ who will take you to the deeper and hidden things. The scroll is behind the door because God has set it up that for you to fully fulfill your destiny, it has to be done through Christ Jesus. You have to go through the door of Christ Jesus. He is the way, the truth, and the life and no man pleases the Father but by him. That is why the scripture says that we can do all things through Christ Jesus who strengthens us. Seek by God's spirit and find the door of Jesus Christ.

It is Christ's desire for you to come through the door and partake of his hidden manna but he is waiting for an action from you. The greatest commandment is to love the Lord with all your heart, mind, soul, and strength. This is why the word "knock" is there. The Lord wants to feel your hunger, passion, and desperation in this quest for your destiny. He doesn't want you to tap on the door gently like you are scared of waking up a sleeping baby in the house. No, he wants you with all your heart and strength, to give it all you got and knock on that door like it's the police coming to apprehend a criminal. Pound the door with your love for Christ and his purposes. Let him know you have arrived excitedly anticipating to know your purpose so you can make the Father proud and pleased.

Right Motive and Priority

Ephesians 1 (KJV)

17 That the God of our Lord Jesus Christ, the Father of glory, may give unto you the spirit of wisdom and revelation in the knowledge of him (relationship):
18 The eyes of your understanding being enlightened; that ye may know what is the hope of his calling (revelation), and what the riches of the glory of his inheritance in the saints,

Before we move forward, I want to key in on something as a word or encouragement and caution. In our quest for the knowledge of the testimony

52

scrolls of destiny, our priority must be intimacy with God. Our motive must be out of love with the desire to please him. Let nothing else be the reason why we are pursuing this. If our motive is wrong, it might cause us to receive the wrong information or open the door for the enemy to come in and lead us astray. Our priority must be the Most High above all our desires and needs. Some may say of course that is what our motive and desire is. But sometimes, our own agendas and aspirations can come into the picture. We might just be seeking so we can be successful for our own sakes or to look good before others. We might see what is on the scroll and say I only accept part of it and then try to fulfill a mixture of what is on the scroll and what we want to accomplish. This is the testimony scroll of destiny designed and written by the Father according to his plan and counsel. His desire is for us to align to that. The desire to do the complete will of God should be the centerpiece of our pursuit of destiny.

I highlighted the scripture above again because there is so much truth in it. It is key. I can't repeat it enough. The prayer is asking for the spirit of wisdom and revelation. What happens is that some just want the spirit of wisdom and revelation just so they can see. They basically get high off of spiritual insight and vision and the matter of doing the will goes out of the Father goes out the window. But the verse lets us know the number one reason what the spirit of wisdom and revelation is for. It is for the "knowledge" of God. It is for the intimate knowing of the Father and Son. This is pertinent information because now we see a pattern here. It is through the intimacy with the Father and Son that our spiritual eyes within can be filled with light so we can fully align with the destiny ordained for our lives. Be sure that the eyes within can be filled with something that looks like light but it is darkness from the enemy so you can fulfill his purposes. I want to summarize this by stating that relationship with God breeds revelation and responsibility. Out of intimacy, vision will be birthed and a responsibility fueled by love will come front and center so a full grown offspring can come into being. May the words of our mouth and the true mediation of our heart be acceptable in the sight of the Lord.

Clues Along the Pathway

I was not a big student of all the nursery rhymes out there when I was a kid. But one comes to mind that makes me think about our journey to find our scroll of destiny. That is Hansel and Gretel. There is a part where they were led into the woods but they did not want to get lost and wanted to make their way back home. So they decided to leave breadcrumbs so they can follow the trail back home. In their case, the birds ate the breadcrumbs and they got lost which brought them to a very sticky situation. In our case, besides us pursuing the destiny scrolls within our heart, God has left some breadcrumbs around the world that give us indicators of the destiny in our lives and that we are on the right track. The birds of the enemy try to eat them but God is always a step ahead.

Sometimes the clues left are subtle and we have to pay attention. We might hear someone talking, or reading a book and the words seem to resonate in us in a familiar way. We can't shake the feeling that this is important. This is a destiny indicator. Also, of course, we are not going to reach our destiny alone but there are other people we will work with to reach the goal. These are strategic divine connections that are needed. In this case, when we come across these people that we have aligned destinies with, you will have that inner witness that I am connected to this person. These clues are not always obvious so that is why you have to really pay attention to the signs.

You might be reading the bible and you touch a certain scripture and it is like the whole world stands still for a second and the inside of you goes "Bing! Bing! Bing!". You know it is for you. Another scenario is hearing a preacher preach a message and the whole time it feels like they are talking to you and you feel a fire burning in your heart. That is the deepness of God speaking to the deepness within your heart and you feel the link and the pull of it. The other case which I know you can relate to is when you are in a situation and you have this feeling like I have been here before or I have seen this before.

We call it deja vu moments but I believe these are times showing us that we are spiritual beings who have seen this before on some level before we were on the earth. These are to name a few. I mentioned these as scenarios that can happen to anyone, even a person who does not know Jesus. How much more clarity can we walk in concerning our destinies when we are walking in relationship with God of Eternity?

Keys To Finding & Unraveling

This chapter's purpose was to give a platform to start the process of searching for the testimony scroll with you. It was to get you started by using a key scripture as a launchpad to get into the game. So you began to ask, then seek, then knock on the door to finally find the scroll. If you have seen a scroll before, usually it is rolled up and has to be unraveled. I know it is like that big box that you open and a smaller box is inside and then you open that box and then another box is there. And the pattern continues. But know if you persevere and don't give up, you shall obtain it. In future chapters, we will talk about the below seven keys of finding and unraveling the scroll in more detail.

1. Faith
2. Holy Spirit
3. Jesus Christ
4. Circumcision of the Heart
5. Prayer
6. Fasting
7. Ascension

These are vital as key concepts to understand and utilize to reach the finish line of knowing what is on your scroll. But as stated before, knowing is half the battle. You have to take what you know and walk in obedience to what God is calling you to know matter what the price. There is a scripture that relates that we are to work out our own salvation with fear and trembling. I believe the fear here is also referencing a reverence that we should have to our heavenly Father to be obedient to him. But also have a trembling, knowing that we want to make sure to be in line with him because we don't want to miss out on everything he has for us. And missing out can have some serious consequences. Keep in mind that as you seek to find and unravel the scroll of destiny just for you, that there is an enemy who wants to stop you at all cost. Be vigilant and fight the good fight of faith.

Exercise

Before, in previous chapters, I ended with a prayer, but some chapters will end with exercises.

Grab a pen and paper or something to record words with. Position yourself in your placement of prayer. You might want to praise or worship first. But when you get to the point where you are ready, pray the following words of Ephesians 1:17:18.

"Father of glory, I pray that you may give me the spirit of wisdom and revelation in the knowledge of you that I may know you intimately and from that intimacy that the eyes of my heart be filled with understanding and enlightenment that I may know in detail what is the hope of your calling for my life. In Jesus name. Amen."

After you pray this a number of times out loud, then be quiet and still for about 5 to 10 minutes and pay intently inside for particular words that might come to mind. Write those words down. And if you see any images come to mind, write those as well. If this is the first time you have done something like this, continue every day, and trust me you will begin to hear something or see something eventually.

Chapter 5 : FAITH IS A TESTIMONY

* * *

It is very interesting that we have been told as believers to fight the good fight of faith. We are in a war with the enemy and the tool and key of faith is vital to our survival. It is listed as one of the weapons in Ephesians 6 that can be utilized as a shield. A shield is defensive and offensive in nature. You can either block something or you can push the shield to advance and knock something down or push it back. There is a lot of teaching surrounding faith and the different types which is very needed. Some people talk of saving faith. Some think about faith as not going by what you see. Some will key in on that faith without works is dead. Some think of faith as just believing so you can receive. These are all facets of faith. And there are many facets to this topic. But I want us to look at faith from an eternal perspective instead of what I can use right now temporal and earthly perspective.

I want us to see faith that it is a testimony. That faith is a record and a witness in the earth and in us that is eternal and filled with the substance of heaven. Instead of looking at faith from the lens of I am believing God for a new car, let's look at faith from a skyscraper level to see a bigger picture. The picture of a complicated eternal plan of destinies intertwined to bring about an ultimate goal of the Father in the earth. It has been stated in the book of

Revelation, that we overcome the enemy by the blood of the lamb and the word of our testimony. And then we are admonished to fight with faith. If the word of our testimony and faith both deals with war and fighting, then there must be a link with faith and the word of our testimony. There is... Faith is a testimony.

The Measure of Faith

Romans 12 (KJV)

*2 And be not conformed to this world: but be ye transformed by the renewing of your mind, that ye may prove what is that good, and **acceptable, and perfect, will of God.***

*3 For I say, through the grace given unto me, to every man that is among you, not to think of himself more highly than he ought to think; but to think soberly, according as **God hath dealt to every man the measure of faith.***

4 For as we have many members in one body, and all members have not the same office:

5 So we, being many, are one body in Christ, and every one members one of another.

*6 **Having then gifts differing according to the grace that is given to us**, whether prophecy, **let us prophesy according to the proportion of faith;***

7 Or ministry, let us wait on our ministering: or he that teacheth, on teaching;

8 Or he that exhorteth, on exhortation: he that giveth, let him do it with simplicity; he that ruleth, with diligence; he that sheweth mercy, with cheerfulness.

From an eternal bigger picture perspective, faith is more than just believing for something to manifest in your life. It is something that God has placed in you before you could ever believe for something and before you even receive the word of salvation. In the passage above, if we look at verse 3, we are instructed to don't think of ourselves higher than any other person because

God has dealt to every man the measure of faith. I used to think from this scripture, that we all started off with the same level of faith but from verse 6, I see that we have different proportions of faith given to us. And by the context, it is given to us according to our purpose. The whole context of the beginning of Romans 12, is purpose and destiny. There is a connection to the measure of faith that God has dealt to every man and testimony scrolls of destiny.

Let's view in more detail of Romans 12 starting at verse 2. We say all the time that with faith, we don't go by what we see. So verse 2 starts off that we should not be conformed or shaped to this world, but be transformed in our thinking so we can prove what is the perfect and acceptable will of God. So right there, a tone around destiny is set mentioning proving what is the will of God. Then straight away , faith being dealt to every man is brought up. Then it swings to we are one body in Christ being different members with different offices and positions. Can you say destiny? From there, it mentions that we have been given different gifts or disbursements of faith according to the election of grace. Then it goes on to say some are called to prophesy, minister, teach, exhort, give, rule, and show mercy. And from these different aspects, we should do it according to the proportion of faith given us.

I am telling you as much as Christ is the light that lights every man that comes into the world resulting in a spark of light at conception, God has placed in the heart of man a measure of faith at conception. This measure of faith is not so much initially about believing as much as it is with purpose, gifting, and destiny. The word faith in the Greek is "pistis" and it means persuasion or conviction. Have you ever heard someone say, "He is of this persuasion" or "He has this conviction". It is literally placing that person in a certain grouping or category. This is what the measure of faith is doing in you. It is placing you in a certain grouping and calling in God. This eternal faith placed in you is a record from heaven containing a roadmap on how to please God. Faith is a testimony or witness of God's will concerning you.

When a person gets saved, they are agreeing with that witness within them that God ordained salvation for them. Then a person who has "faith in" something, is aligning with what God has already ordained for them.

There is a book I heard of by Dr. Frederick K.C. Price called "Faith, Foolishness, or Presumption". The premise is that everything we call faith is not faith but can fall in the categories of foolishness or presumption. There is a passage that explains that faith comes by hearing and hearing by the word of God. In a shorter version, faith comes by the Word and will of God. True faith is linked to the will of God and not our own desires and aspirations. We should not just name and claim everything we can if it is not based on the will of God, word of God, or the rights we have as a believer. Otherwise, we will be working in foolishness and not be able to defeat the enemy because our faith has no backing from God.

Faith is Substance and Evidence

Hebrews 11 (KJV)
1 Now faith is the **substance of things hoped for**, *the evidence of things not seen.*
2 For by it the elders obtained a **good report**.
3 Through faith we understand that the worlds were framed by the word of God,
so that **things which are seen were not made of things which do appear**.

Growing up in the church since a kid, I have heard one chapter hailed as the Faith Hall of Fame and that is Hebrews chapter 11. So with the above passage , we already know it is going to be all about faith. It starts out with that faith is the substance. This brings to memory of my college days where in the commons area, you could see debates about scriptures happening as different religious sects were trying to prove their points. And one guy who I actually went to high school with was what they called a "5 percenter Muslim" and he would say "Faith is a substance. It is something you can feel.

61

It is tangible". He would say this to combat Christians to say why are you believing in something you can't feel. I thought this was a weak argument since the next part says and evidence of things not seen. What he did not realize is that it is a substance not originated from this world. You can physically discern this substance by your 5 senses. You have to tap into this from a spiritual place.

This substance is heavenly and he has been sent to the earth because it is the building block to manifest things that can be seen based on the genetic encoding of this faith substance from heaven. Just like atoms which we can't see with the naked eye are building blocks of matter that we can see. Verse 3 above lets you know that the things which are seen were not made from things that do appear but from a substance that you can't see with your natural eyes. Faith has another origin other than of earth and it is eternal because faith was the building blocks that framed the worlds by the word and will of God.

It is more than just substance but is the substance of things hoped for. God had a hope and expectation and he placed it in a container (scroll) called faith and dealt the measure of it in every man. It is not a substance that is supposed to be used haphazardly but in accordance with the will, intention, and word of God. Faith deals with intention and purpose from an eternal level. This came from above our pay grade. (laugh) This goes in agreement with a scripture that we visited earlier in Psalms 139. In verse 16, David says to God, "thine eyes did see my substance, yet being unperfect; and in the book all my members were written". That substance that God saw in David before he was ever in the world was the God type of faith that deals with destiny. And this substance translated in a book (scroll) that was written concerning all our members or parts of us. The initial faith put in man is a heaven originated substance placed in man as a scroll of things hoped for. It is not yet perfect until the full fruition of it manifests in the earth.

Now moving on to the next phrase of the first verse of Hebrews 11. Faith is the evidence of things not seen. The measure of faith has been placed in man as evidence and proof that we did not start our journey at conception and delivery into this world. But we ancient spirit beings sent from above with a blueprint and spiritual DNA to manifest something marvelous by the design of God himself. When you begin to walk in destiny or you align with God, it is not because you just happen to have an idea or just said let me try this Jesus thing out. No, The measure of faith deep in you began to call out to you and you decidedly to align with it. It is evidence that there is a world that we can't see with natural eyes. It is also evidence that the world we live in and what we manifest is impacted by this unseen world. When you go to court and there is a trial and they want to "convict" a person, evidence must be presented to be a witness or testimony against that person. (Remember , one of the meanings of faith is conviction). The measure of faith in us is a testimony of God that speaks in us if we are looking for it. Our goal is to align our persuasion to the eternal faith of God in us. As his testimony vibrates and speaks in us, we come in agreement with that and believe and speak what he is speaking.

Faith Pleases God

Hebrews 11 (KJV)

4 By faith Abel offered unto God a more excellent sacrifice than Cain, by which he obtained witness that he was righteous, God testifying of his gifts: and by it he being dead yet speaketh.

5 By faith Enoch was translated that he should not see death; and was not found, because God had translated him: for before his translation he had this testimony, that he pleased God.

6 But without faith it is impossible to please him: for he that cometh to God must believe that he is, and that he is a rewarder of them that diligently seek him.

Above are the next 3 verses in which another focus is highlighted with a simple theme of what pleases God. It starts with Abel, that by faith he offered unto God a more excellent sacrifice than Cain. This is because God had communicated what he required and Abel came into alignment with that and his sacrifice was accepted. Cain gave what he wanted to give and it wasn't his best and his sacrifice was denied. In verse 4, I see the same theme that faith is a testimony when it says God testified of his Abel's gift so much so that his faith in obedience still speaks beyond the grave. That is what we desire, faith that speaks for us on the day of judgment beyond the grave. Obviously, by this excellent sacrifice, it pleased God. Next, we have Enoch who by faith was translated to the point where he did not see death. He was so in tune with faith that it translated him from the earthly realm to the spiritual realm where faith originated from. And this translation due to faith was a testimony that he pleased God.

Simply put, faith pleases God. But verse 6, goes to the next level with it. It conveys that it is impossible to please God without faith. That is a strong statement concerning faith. Saying faith pleases God is one thing. Because we can say praise as well as other things can please God as well. But to say it is impossible to please God without a particular thing means for God it is a must have. The reason why it is impossible to please God without faith is because God gave a measure of faith to every man that is embedded with the things that he is expecting for a person to fulfill. If we fulfill the testimony of the end he declared concerning us at the beginning, this pleases the Father. We have to access the testimony of God through faith to hear those words of "Well Done, Good and Faithful Servant". Notice it says, "faithful" servant. The person who pleases him is the one full of faith or should I say it is the person who fulfilled what was in the measure of faith placed in them. He has begun a good work in us by the measure of faith. If we align to his ways and purpose, he will also be pleased to be faithful (full of faith) to complete it.

Another note at the end of verse 6 suggests the fact that the faith in you is a substance and evidence that points you in the direction of God himself.

When we tap into true faith, it draws us to come after God for we now know that he is the great I AM from the beginning. Destiny is the underlying thing that we should be seeking. Our priority and motive is to seek him. Not just seek him in our own timing and with leisure. But the call is for us to seek him diligently with every fiber of our being. The cry of faith in us is to chase after God himself so that we can reap the reward of having a testimony that we pleased God. It is not about heaven. It is not about the mansion in the sky. It is not about having bragging rights of being a perfectionist because you completed everything on your faith scroll. But the aim and target of our pursuit and seeking is God himself. That is why Jesus came into the world so we can be conformed to the image of the Son so we can be reconciled back to the Father.

Faith That Overcomes

1 John 5 (KJV)

*For whatsoever is born of God overcometh the world: and this is the **victory that overcometh the world, even our faith**.*

In my ministry training, my spiritual father always taught me there are three main things that you are supposed to overcome. Those are the enemy, the world, and the flesh. You overcome the enemy by the Word. You overcome the flesh by the Spirit of God. And you overcome the world by faith as we see in the above scripture. (saved through faith. The god of this world is the enemy so if we are to overcome the world, we also have to overcome the enemy.. They are in a sense one in the same. The scripture we started off with in this book is that they overcame the enemy by the blood of the Lamb and the word of their testimony. This seems to check out and make sense. Because faith is a testimony that overcomes the world and the Word overcomes the enemy. So put those together and you have the word of their testimony that defeats the enemy and his world that he arranged to defeat

65

you.

The main goal of the enemy is to kill, steal, and destroy you so you do not make it to the finish line. He wants to disrupt the plan of God for your life. The record of faith in you from the beginning that contains what pleases God is what he wants you to fall short of. But thanks be to God who causes us to triumph because he planted in us the measure of faith to be a substance that can be formed as a weapon to defeat the enemy at any cost. A person who knows their destiny by faith, is a powerful person against the plots and schemes of the enemy. The key is to seek the Father by coming into agreement with the chronicles of faith in you that will cause you to overcome in this fight of faith.

The Scroll of Faith

Hebrews 12 (KJV)
Wherefore seeing we also are compassed about with so great a cloud of witnesses, let us lay aside every weight, and the sin which doth so easily beset us, and let us run with patience the race that is set before us,
2 **Looking unto Jesus the author and finisher of our faith**; who for the joy that was set before him endured the cross, despising the shame, and is set down at the right hand of the throne of God.

The chapter of Hebrews 11 goes on to discuss other champions of faith who pleased God which eventually leads to chapter 12. It begins with the notion that this journey in this life is like a race in which we have to lay aside every sin and weight as we patiently endure it till the finish line. But verse 2 gives us the anecdote of finishing this race. We have to look to Jesus who is the author and finisher of our faith. Some might be wondering why this section is called "The Scroll of Faith". Well faith is a written record of the testimony of God. There has to be a book or scroll for someone to be an author. Authors write things like books, articles, and so on. That measure of faith dealt to us was authored by Jesus Christ before we came into this world. This book contains all our members and what God has destined us for. When we come into this earth, the book has been started but is not complete or finished until we walk it out in the earth. We can only complete or finish this book with the help of Jesus. (We will discuss more in detail in future chapters). Jesus who is the Word as he expressed the will of the Father as he proceeded out of him wrote our scroll of faith that is now a record within us.

There is a scripture that says "the just shall live by his faith". I used to assume that "his" was the human being who was walking in faith. But upon more studying I realized that "his" refers to the ownership of Jesus Christ. He authors and deposits the faith in us at birth in this world. Then we must come in agreement with that faith and from there he can finish it in us as we yield to him in our life. We only can fulfill the destiny assigned to our lives by Christ Jesus. To be honest , none of the faith that contributes to us being more than conqueror is any of ours. It is all his. It is all by him. That should be our desire for it to be all him. We should want our testimony to be that of Galatians 2:20 which states, "I am crucified with Christ: nevertheless I live; yet not I, but Christ liveth in me: and the life which I now live in the flesh , **I live by the faith of the Son of God**, who loved me, and gave himself for me." We should want it on record that it is no longer us who live but we live by the faith of the Son of God. May our banner say that we lived by the scroll faith authored and finished by Jesus Christ himself.

Saved by Grace Through Faith

Ephesians 2 (KJV)
*8 For by **grace are ye saved through faith;** and that not of yourselves: it is the*

67

gift of God:
9 Not of works, lest any man should boast.
10 For we are his workmanship, created in Christ Jesus unto good works, **which**
God hath before ordained that we should walk in them.

Above is another one of my favorite passages in the bible. Part of my mandate on my scroll is to teach about his grace. You can't talk about scrolls, destiny, or things from an eternal perspective without talking about grace. So I will try my best to not go so deep into the aspects of grace. If I had to define grace I would say that it is the supernatural endowment of God in you to empower you to fulfill the will of God in your life. Some people confuse mercy and grace as the same things but my distinction to those two are that they are two sides of a coin but not the same. Mercy is God coming down in us and seeing things from our eyes. Grace is us rising up into God to see things through his eyes and perspective. Another way I look at it is that mercy is not getting what you deserve. Grace is getting what you don't deserve because the election of grace happens before you came to earth before you did any work to qualify or disqualify you for that destiny and the giftings that come along with it.

Romans 9 (KJV)

*11 (**For the children being not yet born**, **neither having done any good or***
***evil**, that the **purpose of God according to election** might stand, **not of works**,*
*but of him that **calleth**;)*
12 It was said unto her, The elder shall serve the younger.
*13 As it is written, **Jacob have I loved, but Esau have I hated**.*

The above shows an example of Jacob and Esau going through the election of grace before they were even born on the earth. It was not based on works but on who God chose. When it says he hated Esau, it does not mean in the way that we think. In the Greek, the word "hated" really means that another was preferred before that person and therefore that person was rejected for that calling. Grace has nothing to do with our works and accolades on the earth but it is linked to a calling that we were ordained to walk in before the foundation of the earth. We are saved by grace through faith because salvation deals more with the destiny we received before we were here than us believing in Christ so we can just go to heaven.

Someone can still get to heaven if they don't fully finish their destiny by the blood of the Lamb. But God is calling us to a high calling and a full salvation. The goal is to finish the course and overcome so we can inherit the kingdom of God not just be able to make it to heaven. Inheriting the kingdom of God and making it to heaven are not the same thing. It is recorded in the bible that he or she who overcomes will have a chance to sit with him on his throne and reign with him. There are different levels and rewards based on how you fare here on earth. Another witness in the bible that salvation is linked to testimony of faith that was given you is in ! Peter 1:9. This conveys that you receive the full reward of glory and joy unspeakable when you come to the end of your faith which is the true salvation of your soul. We have to allow Jesus to finish the scroll of faith in us as we complete fully everything that was on the record of faith placed in us. Every box has to be checked so we can truly say we are at the end of our faith and achieved full salvation of our souls. This will allow us to hear "Well Done, Good and Faithful Servant". There is another scripture that says those are saved who endured till the end. I used to read that and think if I endure and stay in Christ till the end , then I am okay. But now I see another aspect. I must endure to the end of my faith. I must finish the race charted for me to walk in the full salvation that is by grace through faith. The finish line is to have the testimony that we overcame the enemy and world by the faith of the Son of God.

Prayer

Abba Father of Heaven, I come to you and I ask that you cause a new stir within the reader to align with the faith that was placed in them from the beginning. Cause them to read and hear of its contents. Cause them to by faith to have a testimony that they pleased you. I pray that you bring them to a place where they are crucified with you that they no longer live by their agendas and dictates but live by the faith of the Son of God. In Jesus Name, Amen.

Chapter 6 : THE HOLY SPIRIT HAS A TESTIMONY

* * *

The Most High is so marvellous in all his ways. It is said that we were fearfully and wonderfully made. This means he took his time and was very strategic in the implementation of his plan for us. He had to place stepping stones in position to ensure success. Some of these stepping stones were the testimony scroll of destiny (the measure of faith), the Holy Spirit, and Jesus Christ. Some might wonder why he needed all these parties to be in position. The answer is two fold. First he needs witnesses with testimony and second they all play their part. There is an eternal spiritual principle we need to explore.

The Torah, which some refer to as the first five books of the bible, was a shadow and pattern of the principles of God in a concealed matter. It was not until Jesus Christ came on the scene, that the truth of those principles could be fully revealed. In Deuteronomy 19:15, an eternal principle about law and judgment was introduced. It basically explains that before you can judge a person for a particular thing you need two or three witnesses to establish the matter. Jesus also echoes this same principle in Matthew 18:16.

71

Then Paul reiterates the same principle in 2 Corinthians 13:1 where each three times it was applied a little differently. So if God wants his Word to be established by two or three witnesses, then he will not violate his own spiritual principle. Christ is the Word and the measure of faith and the Holy Spirit makes two witnesses. When you come in alignment with the Word, then you become the third witness so the matter can be established before the judgment seat of God.

Some might say why do you break them up into three persons? Aren't they the same person? Without getting in a big debate, the answer is no. The Father is greater than the Son. The Father sent the Son. The Son only does what he has seen the Father does. The Holy Spirit does not speak of himself but speaks of the Son. The Father is on the throne in heaven now with the Son sitting at his right hand while the Holy Spirit has been poured out on all flesh. They are so in tune they are one but they are three. Some choose to look at the one side of the equation and some choose to look at the three side of the equation. I like to view it from the three persons perspective just to show the different functions of them. It is like looking under the hood to see the mechanics of one car moving in one direction.

I brought this up because they are witnesses and a testimony of each other. The Son is the witness of the Father. The Holy Spirit is the witness of the Son. In the halls of eternity, the Son was in the Father as a witness of his will and intention. As he proceeded out of the Father as the manifested Word, books were written into scrolls in eternity. The Holy Spirit was there as a witness of that Word and those scrolls which ended up as measures of faith within mankind. Because the Holy Spirit had a front row seat, he has an eyewitness account and witness of your destiny and therefore has a testimony concerning you.

Helps Our Infirmities

Romans 8 (KJV)

*24 **For we are saved by hope**: but hope that is seen is not hope: for what a man seeth, why doth he yet hope for?*

*25 **But if we hope for that we see not**, then do we with patience wait for it.*

*26 Likewise **the Spirit also helpeth our infirmities**: for we know not what we should pray for as we ought: but the Spirit itself maketh intercession for us with groanings which cannot be uttered.*

*27 **And he that searcheth the hearts knoweth what is the mind of the Spirit**, because **he maketh intercession for the saints according to the will of God.***

Even though we were in the Father before the foundation of the world and witnessed certain things, when we came into the earth, we were covered with a veil of forgetfulness. That veil was not necessarily there at the start. Babies still remember eternity and who they are but as they continue to acclimate to this world they forget. And so when we get here, we forget where we came and who we are and also because of the fall, we are spiritually dead as well. We are in a place where we are weak and need help. The Holy Spirit is the helper we need. He is our comforter, standby, advocate and most importantly our helper.

As the passage above in verse 24, we are saved by hope which means we have an expectation of full salvation. What full salvation is and the reality of it in the beginning of our salvation journey is not fully manifested before eyes. We don't have the full details. Before accepting Christ as our savior and Lord, we are dead spiritually. We need the Holy Spirit to get the party started. He is the catalyst that breathes in us to make us born again spiritually by the Spirit. Then as an infant born again spirits, we can't see clearly. We are still learning our new spiritual surroundings and need the assistance of the Holy

Spirit in our blindness to lead us and point us to the Christ within and our destiny scroll hidden in our heart. We are so clueless, we don't even know what to pray for and need the Holy Spirit to help us pray for the perfect will of God for our lives. We, as verse 27 suggests, need to make a determination to seek our heart so we know what the mind of the Spirit is. Thanks be to the Almighty, he placed the Holy Spirit in our lives while even when we feel helpless, he is there. He will never leave us or forsake us.

His Witness Causes Us To Be Witnesses

Romans 8 (KJV)
*16 The Spirit itself beareth **witness with our spirit, that we are the children of God:***

Acts 1 (KJV)
*8 But ye shall receive power, **after that the Holy Ghost is come upon you: and ye shall be witnesses unto me** both in Jerusalem, and in all Judaea, and in Samaria, and unto the uttermost part of the earth.*

The Holy Spirit is very vital in the process of us awakening to the reality of who we are. The Holy Spirit has a testimony from eternity and we need him to testify some very important things to our spirit man. This is something we can't receive with our natural mind. We have to understand it from our spirit man because the natural man can't fully comprehend things that should be spiritually discerned. One thing that the Holy Spirit is going to testify and be a witness to according to Romans 8:16 is that we are the children of God. This is more than just we are now born again and we can just live a nice happy saved life. It goes deeper. The Holy Spirit is witnessing to us that we are children of God with God's DNA who came out of eternity with a destiny and purpose. You might be wondering how I know that. I know because in the context of this scripture, later down the chapter, Apostle Paul begins to talk about the sons of God are the ones who are led by the Holy Spirit. Then he elaborates further that God foreknew us and called, justified, and glorified us before the foundation of the world. If we have the Holy Spirit and really are listening to his testimony, he is witnessing that you are a child of the Most High God who has a calling.

The Holy Spirit has another component to his testimony and witness. Not only was he there in the beginning to reveal who we are. He was there in the beginning to reveal who the Son of God is. Scripture lets us know that the Holy Spirit will not speak of himself, but will testify of the Son. Acts 1:8 above reiterates this sentiment, as Jesus is speaking, to let them know that you need the Holy Spirit (Ghost) to come upon you so you can be a witness of him. Because we have the Holy Spirit and he has a testimony of Jesus Christ, he can lead us to a place where we are witnesses of Jesus Christ having the same testimony. Revelation lets us know that the saints will have the testimony of Jesus Christ. What is that? It goes on to say that the spirit of prophecy which is the Holy Spirit is the testimony of Christ. There it is. The purpose of the Holy Spirit is to witness and reveal Jesus Christ to us.

I believe an interesting thing that sticks out to me is that Jesus Christ in Acts is talking to disciples who have been with him for three and a half years observing everything about him. So from a natural and temporal perspective that had an eyewitness account of Jesus Christ. But this was not enough, the Holy Spirit had to come to bring a fuller testimony in view. This testimony and witness is from an eternal and spiritual perspective. We no longer can know Christ by the flesh and by words we read. We have to know him by the witness of the Holy Spirit so we can indeed be true witnesses of Christ.

The Teacher

1 John 2 (KJV)

27 But the anointing which ye have received of him abideth in you, and ye need not that any man teach you: **but as the same anointing teacheth you of all things, and is truth,** *and is no lie, and even as it hath taught you, ye shall abide in him.*

The Holy Spirit helps our infirmities, causes us to be witnesses unto Christ, and he also is a teacher for us. He is the spirit of truth and he is there to teach us truth from the beginning. The above passage shows us that we don't even need a man to teach since the anointing (Holy Spirit) will teach you all things. It is not that we don't need other men or women of God to teach us. We know this because one of the fivefold ministry gifts is the teacher. But any true teacher of the fivefold should be pointing you to the Holy Spirit and be teaching you by the upper teacher who is the Holy Spirit. What the Holy Spirit needs to teach you must be grabbed by your spirit man. There is a possibility that if another human being teaches you, you might just grab it with your natural mind. But while a natural man is teaching you still need to listen to the inner teacher who abides in you to feed and grow your spirit man.

The Holy Spirit is the first person of the process. It is like when you go to school. School is not the main event, but it prepares you to be able to handle the main event in the real world. This is what the Holy Spirit is doing. He is preparing the way as a forerunner for Christ. You have to be prepared to know the Christ in you. You can't come just any type of way. He is a king. This reminds me of the book of Esther. You had the king who was looking for a bride. Many women came to be the bride but all did not qualify. They had to go through schooling and training under the tutelage of the eunuch. The eunuch was someone the king could trust who would not taint the bride in training and take away the attention from the king as the main focus. At times they will have little moments with the king to see if he approved of their progress. They would have to soak in oils for months for purification. Jesus Christ is the king that we are betrothed to waiting for full union with him. The Holy Spirit is the eunuch teaching us to prepare us for the king by also soaking us in his oil to purify us. The Holy Spirit knows what the king likes and they work together to get us where we need to be.

The inner teacher in us is there to teach us all things that pertain to Christ and ourselves. One of the characteristics of the Holy Spirit that intrigues me is that he will bring all things to remembrance of what Christ has said to us before per John 14:26. The context is to the disciples but once again, some of the disciples are taking notes while Jesus is teaching and probably had pretty decent memories. I believe this scripture speaks deeper that there are some things from an eternal and spiritual plane that you need to be awakened to by the Holy Spirit that I spoke to you before you were even on the earth. And then another scripture says that the Holy Spirit will show us things to come. The Holy Spirit possesses a testimony of eternity of things that have been ordained before the foundation of the earth that enables him to show us things to come concerning our destiny and the world. From experience, I am so thankful that we have an unction from God abiding in us who teaches us and prepares us.

Leads Us To Christ

Before Jesus Christ manifested in the earth, he had a forerunner of John the Baptist who was a witness declaring "Repent for the kingdom of God is at hand". That was one witness and then Jesus Christ after he is baptized by John the Baptist, comes back from being tried in the wilderness with the same witness and message. "Repent for the kingdom of God is at hand".

Then Christ disciples after being given authority over the enemy are sent to the lost house of Israel with the witness and message, "Repent for the kingdom of God is at hand. God's process is to have his word established by two or three witnesses. This was done on earth.

Now moving to the inner spiritual view, the Holy Spirit is in us and Christ is in us. One is the forerunner to prepare the way for the other. The goal is for the Holy Spirit to testify the witness of heaven to us and lead us to the Christ in us who will echo the same testimony from heaven. This will eventually lead to us being like the disciples where we began to repeat the same testimony and witness that we received from Christ and the Holy Spirit by our spirit man. That is why after Christ we are a new creation and we no longer live by the flesh, we live in and by the spirit. No longer do we proclaim what is from man's wisdom but we tap into the streams of revelation that our spirit man has access to. This way we stay connected to the source of truth to reflect and project the truth keeping the testimony intact.

When born again by the Spirit of God, we are infants spiritually. And as a baby depends on its mother and father for everything, we must totally trust and rely on the forerunner to prepare the way to Christ. They have two different functions. The Holy Spirit is the birther, helper, comforter, and teacher. Christ in you is the bridegroom, king, the way, truth, life, and the light. The Holy Spirit only takes you so far, but the witness of Christ is greater. The Holy Spirit is the way to Christ in us while Christ in us is the way to the Father. Concerning your destiny scroll hidden in your heart, the Holy Spirit will lead you to the garden of your heart. But you will need the light of Christ to find it and Christ himself to open and unravel the scroll. The Holy Spirit is the oil that leads to the light of Christ for the spirit of man is the candle of the Lord. The role of a teacher and bridegroom is different.

The Living Water

John 7 (KJV)

38 He that believeth on me, as the scripture hath said, out of his belly shall flow rivers of living water. 39 (But this spake he of the Spirit, which they that believe on him should receive: for the Holy Ghost was not yet given; because that Jesus was not yet glorified.)

There is one more aspect of the Holy Spirit I want to leave you with. He is the living water. Christ says he who comes to me shall never thirst again. You have to come to him by the way of the Holy Spirit to partake of living water. Christ never said he was the living water because he is the living bread. One deals with thirst and another deals with hunger. One is not quite as filling as the other. That is because the realm of the Holy Spirit is not the fullness of what God has for us. The realm of Christ (living bread) is weightier in our spiritual belly than water is. The realm of the Holy Spirit deals with the anointing but the realm of Christ leads you to the glory and fire. But we need both to be satisfied from a thirst and hunger perspective.

Revelation 7:17 shows that Christ is not the living water as it says Christ the Lamb in the midst of the throne will feed us and then lead us to the living fountains of waters. From the hunger side, we are to eat the Passover Lamb and the living bread, then we can wash it down with the living water which is connected to the Holy Spirit. This is evident in Genesis 1 when the Holy Spirit moved upon the waters. This is his domain. Also in John 7:38 above, Christ let us know that to those who believe in him, out of their belly, rivers (not one) will flow. Then the verse goes on to say that Christ spake of the Holy Spirit who will come. The Holy Spirit is the living water that we must drink and be watered by.

In previous chapters, I mentioned that within our heart is a garden. And that the testimony scrolls of destiny are hidden in our heart. Some might have assumed that the garden of our heart is Eden in us. But what if I told you that during the fall of man as paradise and Eden was imploded in man, that a garden was separated for man to dress and keep in this realm we live in spiritually out of Eden to still produce a harvest that will eventually manifest in the natural world. In Genesis 2:10, it shows the pattern that God still intends for the garden of our heart and that is for a river to come "out of Eden" to water a garden that was then split into four rivers. It is interesting that we have 4 chambers of the heart. So without the new birth by the Holy Spirit our way to Eden was cut off but now with the new birth is made open so that the living waters can flow in the garden of our heart.

The subject of the garden of our heart is brought up because our scroll is hidden in this garden. The Holy Spirit's job is to lead us to the garden so that Christ can help us open the scroll. The contents of the scroll are like seeds that then need to be planted in the garden of your heart so that you can grow the right harvest. Out of the abundance of the harvest of your heart, the mouth will speak, and then eventually manifest in the earth. Life and death is in the power of the tongue. Christ opens the scroll and helps us as the husbandman of our garden to sow the seeds in our heart. He also prunes the garden to get rid of the bad stuff. After the seeds are planted, then the Holy Spirit moves upon the rivers of living water, just like in creation, to flow out of Eden on the seeds so they may grow. It has to be water from Eden (heaven in us) because that which is born of spirit is spirit but that which is born of flesh is flesh. It has to be living water or else it will die. One plant, one water, and God gives the increase. We need the living water of the Holy Spirit.

Prayer

Heavenly Father, I pray that you grant the reader to be in position to receive the full function and benefits of the Holy Spirit. May the Holy Spirit be their living breath, comforter, helper, inner witness, teacher , and living water. If they are not baptized by the Holy Spirit with evidence of speaking in tongues, I pray that as they read these words, that the Holy Spirit of heaven will come upon them and activate the flow of the living waters in their belly. I pray that they will be fully led by the Spirit and heed his instruction to walk intimately with Christ. May they continue to pursue their destiny to be pleasing in your sight. In Jesus name. Amen.

Chapter 7 : JESUS CHRIST THE SCROLL OPENER

* * *

Hebrews 12 (KJV)

1 Wherefore seeing we also are compassed about with so great a cloud of witnesses, let us lay aside every weight, and the sin which doth so easily beset us, and let us run with patience the race that is set before us,

2 Looking unto Jesus the author and finisher of our faith; who for the joy that was set before him endured the cross, despising the shame, and is set down at the right hand of the throne of God.

I had the urge to title this chapter "Jesus Christ Superstar" but it did not fit with the theme of scrolls, destiny, or testimonies. He is the morning star and he is super so I was still on the fence with it. Nevertheless, Jesus Christ is so many things. He is the firstborn of creation. He is the express image of the Father. He is the beginning and the ending. He is the savior of mankind. The list can go on and on for days. There is none like him. He is simply in a league of his own because he is the first, the lead, and the head in all ways. He is the ultimate role model and the pattern we should look to for us to triumph in this life as God intended. There are a lot of worldly views of what success and victory are. But true victory in life is doing the will of the Father and being what he created you to be. We were created to be in his image and likeness and be an extension of his will in the earth.

As the above passage has implied, there is a race that is set before us when we came to the earth. With a race like a marathon, you can't just run the race and go in whatever path you want to go to get to the finish line. A course or map has been outlined detailing the course, the checkpoints, markers for different phases, how many laps and other highlighted notes. There are specific rules in the marathon that say you can't ride a bike or utilize a car to get to the finish line. There is a certain way you have to run. In your preparation, you understand there are times when you run your fastest and then there are times you pace yourself. The race analogy has many different symbols that you can grab and link to our journey in life. But the key part is that the way we truly finish this race is that we must keep our eyes on Jesus Christ. He is the way, the truth and the life. He is the pattern, blueprint, and roadmap. We must do all things through Christ. He is the first witness and expression of the intentions and mind of the Father.

First Testimony

Hebrews 1 (KJV)
God, who at sundry times and in divers manners spake in time past unto the fathers by the prophets,
2 Hath in these last days **spoken unto us by his Son,** whom he hath **appointed heir of all things**, by whom also he made the worlds;
3 Who being the **brightness of his glory, and the express image of his person**, and upholding all things by the word of his power, when he had by himself purged our sins, sat down on the right hand of the Majesty on high

The Lord Jesus Christ is the express image of the Father. In other words, he is the full expression of all that the Father is. Jesus himself says when you see him you see the Father. Why is this? It is because he is the first to witness and have a testimony of all that Father is and what he plans to do. It is because of this, that he was considered the firstborn of creation and by him all things were made because he had the original blueprint. Since he is the firstborn of all creation and we know that the greatest inheritance goes to the firstborn, then Jesus Christ is appointed heir to all things. Why was so much pronounced on the Lord Jesus Christ? It is because he held the first testimony of the Father.

In John 1:1 it states, "In the beginning was the Word, and the Word was with God, and the Word was God." So before everything, Christ was the Word, the expression of the will of God that brought forth creation. This came about by him being "with" the Father and through that fellowship and intimacy he became turned into that same image of the Father. This is a spiritual principle. What you look at , you will become. This is the goal of why we need Christ in our lives because as we engage Jesus Christ and he becomes real to us, we can gaze upon him and become the same image. We can gaze at him and see the first and original blueprint and follow that lead so we can finish the race.

Let's focus on Christ being the express image of the Father. Some might look at an image as being a picture but it is so much more. An image if you look deeper is an embedded genetic code along with other brushstrokes and pixels come together to be the finished product of the picture we see. But with an artist, the picture is just the endgame. That artist had planning, intentions, themes, messages, blending of colors that came together to be the image you see. The final picture and image that God wants to see in our lives is Christ. That is what creation for us was all about. The Father said to the Son let "us" make man in our image and likeness. The Father is the original source and the Son is the first witness and testimony. We need that testimony to speak in our lives.

Another aspect of the passage above in verse 2 is that all things are created by Christ the Son. As we discuss the topic of destiny in this book, many of us have certain questions. What are we here for? What is my purpose? A good reporter knows if they want answers and the truth, you have to go to the source. And the further you get from the original source, the more the testimony and truth gets watered down. The source that has been provided to us is Jesus Christ. Let's say someone bought you a super top of the line vacuum cleaner. But you never saw one or never even heard of the term. You don't have a clue what the item before you is or its purpose. This is why most items that are manufactured have an owner's manual. You want to know what and why something is, you go to the creator of that thing. That testimony of who you are and the in depth instructions of how you are supposed to function is in you by Christ Jesus.

Christ In You

Colossians 1 (KJV)
26 Even the **mystery which hath been hid from ages and from generations**, but **now is made manifest to his saints**:
27 To whom God would make known what is the riches of the glory of this mystery among the Gentiles; which is **Christ in you, the hope of glory:**

I believe there are a lot of people who think of Jesus Christ high and seated on a throne in the highest of heavens. This is a marvelous idea to have in your mind and heart concerning Jesus. But sometimes if we have only this view of Jesus, we limit ourselves on the intimacy we can have with him. He is omnipresent which means he is everywhere. When I mention to people that they need to get from Jesus the blueprint of their lives, some frustration comes over them. This is because they are viewing the Lord so far from them and they say how in the world can I get close to him to get the answers I need. The answer is Christ is in you and not far at all.

Romans 10:8 lets us know that the word is near us in our mouth and in our heart. Christ is the Word and he lives in us and is very near to us. Another witness in the bible is in the first chapter of John where it lets us know that Christ is the light that lights every man that comes into the world. This is the mystery that has been hidden from ages in the beginning but Jesus came onto the scene, now this mystery is being revealed. The mystery is that every man has Christ in him or her when they are born. The issue is that we were born in sin and were shaped in iniquity from the womb. We need to be born again by the Spirit of God to be a new creation in the spirit to be able to be aware of the Christ in us. When you see the word "mystery" being used in scripture, that is a key indicator that we need to pay attention. This mystery of Christ in us is key when it comes to intimacy and you fulfilling your destiny.

The other part of the above passage is not only the who but also the why. The who is Jesus Christ and us. But the why is that he lives in us so we can have a hope and trajectory towards glory. There are many dimensions of the word glory here we will focus on honor, riches, and abundance. There is a level of honor that we are supposed to enter into. There is also an arena of abundance that is our portion and inheritance (birthright). When it comes to athletes when they win there is a certain glory they obtain. We are in the race of life and destiny and our desire should be to finish with glory. If there is a war, the winner and overcomer who has grabbed the spoils of war and walks in a type of glory. Our goal should be to walk in overcomer's glory over the enemy. We need to get access to Christ in us, so we can finish the race and walk in the glory of being more than a conqueror.

Before in an earlier chapter, it was discussed more on the fact that Jesus is the author of our faith. He is the author of the book and scroll of faith in us. He is the evidence that is not seen by the physical eyes that lives in us. He is the substance of things hoped for which is in us. Colossians 1:27 answers the question of what we are hoping for. We are hoping for the glory of a finished race to partake in our full inheritance. Yes, the book (scroll) has been authored by Christ in you but as we turn to the Lord, we partner with him so that the book can be finished and manifested in our lives. God who has begun a good work in you is "faithful" to complete it in you. Where is he completing it at? He is completing it "in you" How is he going to complete it? He will do this by the Christ in you who is the author and finisher of your faith which is your testimony scroll of destiny. You can't finish without Christ.

Through Christ

Philippians 4 (KJV)
*13 I can do **all things through Christ** which **strengtheneth** me.*

Hebrews 13 (KJV)
*20 Now the God of peace, that brought again from the dead our Lord Jesus, that **great shepherd of the sheep**, through the blood of the everlasting covenant,*
*21 Make you **perfect in every good work to do his will**, working in you that which is wellpleasing in his sight, **through Jesus Christ**; to whom be glory for ever and ever. Amen.*

The whole way the scheme of things has been engineered is that we must go through Christ Jesus to be where he has called us. I know that there are people who seem to be doing well in life and they feel like they are walking in their destiny. But I tell you the truth, the only way to walk in your full destiny and please God the Father is through Christ Jesus. Jesus came and died for us so we can be reconciled back to the Father from whence we came. He is the only way, the truth, and the life. No man comes to the Father but by him. He is the way that reveals the truth of how and why we live this life. That is why Paul so emphatically said he can do all things through Christ who strengthens him.

The goal is to complete "all things". He does not want us to do just part of what we were destined for in this world but all. On our testimony scrolls there are many items we are to fulfill. We need to do all of them to be tagged with the stamp of "Well done, good and faithful servant". We can only do this through the instruction and strength of God. Why do we need strength? Once again, as a reminder, there is an enemy who wants to stop you at all cost. And there is a war going on whether you like it or not. We need the strength of the Lord Jesus Christ working in us to win the war of destiny. In Ephesians, we are told that it is God who is able to do exceedingly above all we ask or think according to the power that works in us. We need to let the enemy know that our source of power is Christ as we are strong in the power of his might.

Above in verse 20 of Hebrews 13, our heavenly father is referenced as the God of peace. This makes me think of Jeremiah 29:11 where it says that the God of peace does not have evil thoughts concerning us but thoughts of peace to bring us to the expected outcome and destiny. He is at peace because he has a plan through Christ Jesus. The plan was in place from the beginning through an everlasting covenant that we agreed to with God and Christ before we were in our mother's womb. His wisdom put in motion that through Christ the firstborn of creation that he will be the shepherd and bishop of our souls to guide to greener pastures of destiny. This covenant was not started when Christ died for us on the earth 2000 years ago. This covenant did not start when we decided to let Christ in our lives. This is just when we activate the covenant. But the everlasting and eternal covenant was put in effect though the blood of the Lamb who was slain before the foundation of the world. We saw the plan of the infinite Father and said here am I, send me.

The plan was to make us perfect in every good work of his will in our lives. His plan was for us to do all things when it came to the destiny we were foreordained to accomplish. It is the Father's will that all things work out for the good of them who love the Lord and are called according to his purpose. We need the Lord Jesus Christ by our blood covenant and love towards him to walk in the part of all things working out for the good. The good from God's perspective works and plays out in our life when we walk according to his purpose. Verse 21 above aligns with the premise that to be perfect in every good work connected to his will and destiny for lives, we must go through Christ Jesus.

Testimony Bears Testimony

Jesus is the express image and testimony of the Father. God's intent was for us as mankind to walk in his image and his likeness. I have heard some just take that scripture and understand that from a physical perspective. "Well if we are in God's image, then he has a body that looks like ours". That is part of it but it is dealing with "image" and "likeness" and God is a spirit so we must consider his spiritual characteristics as well. In earlier chapters, it was discussed how there is a scroll linked to our physical DNA that is trying its best to smother the frequency of the spiritual DNA of your heavenly Father. This spiritual DNA placed in you in your mother's womb in the form of a destiny scroll has embedded in it everything about you that you are supposed to be when you become a full grown adult. It speaks to your likeness, your spiritual height, your calling, giftings, anointing, and your destiny.

We all are called to be conformed to the image of the Son from a spiritual perspective, but the manifestation of us in this physical plane will be unique like our fingerprints. Just like you can have two parents and they have ten children. If none of these children are identical twins, then they will all be unique in their expression of the mixture of genetics from their parents. Some will differ in gender, complexion, height, likes, interests, talents, and the list goes on. When it comes to our destinies, we have to see it the same way. We are not all called to be in one mold but different expressions of the spiritual DNA of God our father. This is why we should not look at others and want to be exactly like them. We should not look at others and be jealous of who they are becoming. Also, we should not think that we are special because we are walking in a certain destiny and we are looking down on someone else's destiny. We are called according to God's election of grace and we are playing different parts of his creation. But if we are in Christ, we are being an expression of him and his will in the earth.

One of the spiritual characteristics mentioned is height. In Ephesians 4, as Christ was ascending to the Father, he gave gifts to men that some call the fivefold ministry (apostle, prophet, pastor, teacher, evangelist). The purpose of these gifts to the body of believers is for us to come to the full stature (height) of Christ. I just don't see that as being the same height as Christ but I see that as being the height that Christ deemed fit for you personally. When it comes to destiny and spiritual maturity, our perspective should be Christ's perspective and take on it. We should look to him to guide us in our unique given destinies. Jesus holds the testimony of what we are to become. As we engage Jesus and come into contact with that testimony, his testimony (faith) will change us to align with that same testimony. Our testimony then can be his testimony and it wont no longer be our life from the scroll of our physical DNA or our aspirations but we can live by the faith of the Son of God. We can move from bearing the testimony of the enemy and bear the testimony of our creator.

Face To Face

2 Corinthians 4 (KJV)
*6 For God, who commanded the light to shine out of darkness, **hath shined in**
our hearts, to **give the light of the knowledge of the glory of God** in **the face**
of Jesus Christ.*
*7 But we have this **treasure in earthen vessels**, that the excellency of the **power**
may be of God, and not of us.*

Christ is in us so we can be reconciled to God and his plan for us so we can come back to the glory of the Father to claim our full inheritance.We are born again by the breath of the Holy Spirit who will not leave or forsake us. But then the Holy Spirit helps us to search our heart to find Christ in us so we can allow him to sit on the throne of our heart. We can be his domain and treasure possession and his kingdom can reign in us. As Christ our Lord and King, we yield to his pleasures, decrees, and dictates. Jesus is not to be some mythical creature who can't be touched and known by us. We are to engage him within so he can lead and shepherd us in life. This relationship with Jesus is supposed to be intimate, personal and face to face. It is out of our intimacy of our bridegroom that destiny will be birthed in every dimension of our lives.

The above passage lets us know that the light from heaven which is Jesus Christ who lights every man who comes into this world was to shine in the darkness of mankind. It goes on to let us know that this light which is Christ is supposed to shine in our hearts. We need this light to shine because we were born in darkness and could not see. We need the Holy Spirit to birth us again because we were born into this world spiritually blind. Even if we were in the proximity of the light in our heart and we were not born again, we would not see the light. But it is after we are born again with new eyes to see, that the Holy Spirit can condition us and lead us to engage the light which is Christ inside us.

91

This is Christ in us, the hope of glory. This light brings us to a knowledge or intimate knowing of the instructions and blueprint to finish this race of glory. But to do this, we can't have a casual encounter. We must have a never ending bundle of one on one briefing sessions to bring you to a place of revelation of who you are in Christ. This is not some fantasy or figure of speech. There is a place in God that you can walk with Christ in you and know him face to face. This is the beauty of it that Christ in you is the treasure that God placed in you a vessel made of earth so you can find him and give up everything for the pursuit of him. Jesus is the pearl of great price that we are seeking for. It must be done by and through Christ Jesus so that the excellency will be of him and not us. We are saved by grace that not any man should be able to boast. Our quest to finish the race of destiny won't be by our might or by our power but by the spirit of Christ living in us.

I have mentioned the spiritual law which is what we look at is what we will become. Our goal should be to look upon the face of Jesus Christ that is within us. This might be hard to grasp but Christ is in you. It is like a commercial I saw when I was younger about a spaghetti sauce that wanted to make emphasis on the good tomatoes and herbs in it. The company had a slogan of "It's in there". I am telling you now that the goodness and person of Christ is in you and he wants you to find him and taste and see that the Lord is good. It is in the face of Jesus that resides in you and you are being called to face to face relationship with the savior of the world himself.

2 Corinthians 3 (KJV)
16 Nevertheless when it shall turn to the Lord, the vail shall be taken away.
17 Now the Lord is that Spirit: and where the Spirit of the Lord is, there is liberty.
18 But we all, with open face beholding as in a glass the glory of the Lord, are changed into the same image from glory to glory, even as by the Spirit of the Lord.

You might wonder if you have not experienced Christ in this way, is it even possible to engage in such a way. Some people are looking for him at a certain church. Some are looking for him at a conference. Some are even looking for him at a certain holy spot in a particular state in a particular country. But Christ says some false people will say "Lo, he is here and he is there" but the kingdom of God is within you. And we must look and turn inward and find the Christ that lives in us. The Holy Spirit and the spirit of Christ (Lord) are different persons dwelling in you with different purposes. You must ask the Holy Spirit to prepare you and lead you to the place to engage Christ in you who has everything that pertains to life and godliness. He has the key that will lead you to life and life more abundant. He possesses the code that brings you out of the destiny of the fleshly life into the realm of God's ordained destiny for your life. The secret as suggested by the above passage is to turn to the Lord because Jesus the Lord is that spirit. And where that spirit is there is liberty because who the Son has set free is indeed to walk in his calling. Jesus is the truth and the truth shall make you free.

When we come into contact with the Spirit of Jesus , the Christ in us, the vail and scales are removed. Now the veil that has blocked me since my physical birth can be removed and the face and eyes of my heart can not behold openly the face of the Christ within. And we can behold his glory which contains the light and instructions so we can be changed into the image that was ordained before the foundation of the world for us to become. Through continual communion we can keep on getting glimpses of the glory that will lead us to every phase of our destiny. We will move from glory to glory so we can move from phase to phase of our destiny. A face to face relationship with Christ (inwardly and eventually outwardly) causes us to behold the record of eternity he holds to lead us to a fulfilled destiny.

Opener of the Seals

Revelation 5 (KJV)

*1 And I saw in the right hand of him that sat on the throne **a book written*** *within and on the backside, sealed with seven seals.*

*2 And I saw a strong angel proclaiming with a loud voice, **Who is worthy to open the book, and to loose the seals thereof?***

3 And no man in heaven, nor in earth, neither under the earth, was able to open the book, neither to look thereon.

*4 And I wept much, because **no man was found worthy to open and to read the book, neither to look thereon.***

*5 And one of the elders saith unto me, Weep not: behold, **the Lion of the tribe of Judah, the Root of David, hath prevailed to open the book, and to loose the seven seals thereof.***

*9 And they sung a new song, saying, Thou art worthy to take the book, and to open the seals thereof: for thou wast slain, and hast **redeemed us to God** by thy blood out of every kindred, and tongue, and people, and nation;*

*10 And hast made us unto our God **kings and priests:** and we shall reign on the earth.*

I love the book of Revelation and I love the different degrees and facets of the bible can be revealed to us. I believe the book of Revelation particularly speaks to us from different perspectives. It speaks to us literally and symbolically. It speaks to us from an eternal, end time, and a right now perspective. It speaks to us from an outward and an inner perspective. It speaks from an universal, corporate body of Christ, and individual perspective. I say all of this to say that the above passage someone may read and understand it to talk about the end time when Christ comes back to the whole world outwardly and universally. But I want us to look at this passage from an inwardly and individual perspective of Christ coming and revealing himself to us right now. The book of Revelation is about the revelation (unveiling) of Jesus Christ. That can be to the world as a whole and to us individually. Our God is great and beyond us that he can speak to different dimensions and realms at the same time using the same words.

The revelation of Jesus Christ must be unveiled to us and in us. We might ask and it is given. Then we have to seek and find. Then we have to knock so the door can be open. Jesus Christ is that door but behind that door is the book and scroll that contains your destiny and it has seals on it that must be opened. All these seals will not be opened at one time. Some of these seals are for different seasons in your life. Just like certain chapters of this book and scroll must be read in order to understand the full story. No man in his own strength can open the seals of this scroll but we must do it through Christ because he is the one who strengthens us. Oh we need the power of the Lion of Judah, the root of David who has conquered the grave to open the seals of the scroll of destiny in our heart. And it must be done in his timing as well.

There is a book in you and Jesus has the key and the strength to open and unravel it for you to see. He is the light that will shine to the parts you need to see for that particular season in your life. He is the way who reveals the truth. We do not get to the place for finishing the quest of destiny without Jesus Christ. This is apparent in verse 9 above when the redeemed of the Lord began to sing a song declaring that because Christ was worthy to open the seals of the book, they are now redeemed to God. There is no full redemption to God without Christ opening the seals of the testimony scrolls of destiny within you. Verse 9 highlights that we are redeemed by the blood and by the opening of the seals of the book in us. This correlates to another scripture that we started the book with: that we overcame the enemy and we are redeemed by the blood of the Lamb and the Word of "their" testimony.

Oh the wonders of the Lord Jesus Christ. He is truly the superstar of our whole story. It is all about Jesus and without him we are nothing. In him we must live, breathe, and have our being. We must bear his testimony from the eternity of the Father so we can bear the same testimony in our lives. We must seek Christ in us so he is our light and guide. And so he can unlock and open the seals of our scrolls of destiny in our hearts. Our heart's desire must be to have a face to face relationship with Jesus because he is the key to

95

it all. Let this be your main pursuit to find that pearl of great price so you can bring worth and purpose to your life. May the true revelation of Jesus in you bring the revelation of your destiny.

Prayer

Abba Father, I pray that all who are reading this book will walk first in an intimacy with the Holy Spirit and that the Holy Spirit will lead them to the Christ within them. I pray that their inner man will heed the call of Christ in them and turn inward to the Lord. I pray that the face of Christ will be revealed in them and bring such a light of revelation to them concerning their destiny. I pray that Christ will begin to open the seals of the scrolls in their lives and that Christ will sit on the throne of their hearts. May they count the cost first and die to everything else so the life of Christ will flourish in their lives. In the name of Jesus Christ. Amen.

Chapter 8 : CIRCUMCISION OF THE HEART

* * *

Proverbs 4 (KJV)

23 Keep thy heart with all diligence; for out of it are the issues of life.

The heart of man is very special to God. That is why we see in the above passage we are admonished to keep our heart with much diligence. That is why in another scripture we are told if we pray and make our requests known that the peace of God will come and guard our heart and mind. God's heart is after heart. We should not take it lightly. Our posture should be to guard and keep our heart with all that we can do for out of it is the issues of life. That word "issues" in the Hebrew is the the word "towtsaah" which mean a source of which a going out occurs or a fountain that something flows from. Our heart must be guarded because it is the source that life or death, good or evil, can flow from. I believe that Jesus Christ came on the scene to do more than forgive our sins but also unlock something deep inside us so he can possess our heart. He wants more than us to just do good works but he wants the inside nature of our heart to be clean and unhindered in releasing his love and his life in the world. The scroll of destiny is hidden within our heart and to get to the place where we understand some aspects of our heart so we can engage in the process of revealing the treasure inside us.

What is the Heart?

Romans 8 (KJV)

*27 And he that searcheth the hearts knoweth what is the **mind of the Spirit**, because he maketh intercession for the saints according to the will of God.*

In 1 Samuel 16, Samuel was told by God to go to the house of Jesse to anoint the next king of Israel. When Samuel arrived he looked at the oldest and said for sure this is the one but God let him know that he does not look at things the way does. God looks at the heart. I believe God looks at the heart not just because of the posture and intentions of the heart at that time. But he also looked at the scroll that he placed in our hearts and the destiny that is outlined in the scroll within the heart. He looked at David's heart and saw the heart of a king because that destiny was embedded in his heart from the beginning of the earth. Through the election of grace in eternity, this destiny was assigned to David. That is why the heart is so important because everything that pertains to your life and destiny is there. Out of the heart is the issues and flow of everything that makes you you and points you to the God given life that he ordained for your life.

So some might be wondering what really is the heart? I have heard many theories and definitions but I have to trust what the Holy Spirit reveals to me and also what scriptures confirm. The above scripture in Romans 8 reveals that in simple terms, that the heart is the "mind of the spirit" man. First, if the "s" of "spirit" is supposed to be a capital "S" or a lowercase "s". If it is lowercase, then you are seeing that you search the heart because it is the mind of your spirit. If it is supposed to be a capital "S", then I got you from that perspective because in the heart is the mind of the Holy Spirit to the born again believer. It lets you know that the heart is spiritual and if so, then if the mind of the Holy Spirit is revealed in our hearts and our spirit is patterned after the spirit of God, then the heart is shown to be the mind of the spirit man. So either way you go with it, it leads you to that the heart is the mind of the spirit man.

I also want to note that the person in the above scripture searching the heart is not the Holy Spirit as I once believed. If it was the Holy Spirit , why would he be searching your heart to see what his own mind is. The truth is that we ourselves should be searching our own heart. Why? So we can find and unravel the scroll of destiny in our hearts. We have to realize this is a journey and quest and that the scroll is not just plainly in sight. We must search it out of course with the help of the Holy Spirit and Jesus Christ who is the Christ and light in us, the hope of glory.

The Heart Thinks

Proverbs 23 (KJV)
*7 For as he **thinketh in his heart**, so is he: Eat and drink, saith he to thee; but his heart is not with thee.*

Genesis 6 (KJV)
*5 And God saw that the wickedness of man was great in the earth, and that every imagination of **the thoughts of his heart** was only evil continually.*

Matthew 15 (KJV)

99

18 But those things which proceed out of the mouth come forth from the heart; and they defile the man.
19 For out of the heart proceed evil thoughts, *murders, adulteries, fornications, thefts, false witness, blasphemies:*

So this might be a surprise to you!!!! The heart of man is a thinking mechanism. If the heart is the "mind of the spirit man", then it will think and have thoughts. As the above scriptures show, and these are only a few, that thinking and thoughts are related to the heart in scripture. If you do a word search in the bible on "heart" and "think" or "thoughts", a nice amount of scriptures show up to testify to this fact. I know what some are thinking. Don't we think with our brain? Isn't our mind linked to our brain? These are good questions and the answer is yes but there is more to the story. Remember, we are three parts. We are spirit, soul, and body. What if I told you that those three parts, your physical body, your soul, and your spirit man have their own minds and thinking compartments. If part has its own realm to garner information from and process. The physical realm information goes to the brain. The spiritual realm information goes to the heart for processing. And the soulish realm goes to the gut for processing.

The Realms of Man	The Mind of that Realm
Physical (Body)	Brain
Soulish	Gut
Spiritual (Spirit man)	Heart

The Different Areas of Thinking

100

Each realm has a body linked to us. If you were to see your spirit man and soulish man, it is shaped like your physical body on some level. And even though your physical body has a gut and a heart that has its own purpose in the physical body for health, these organs have a link to the soulish and spiritual realm. The physical body is conscious of the earth realm. The soulish body is conscious of yourself. Your soul is the part that makes you unique and an individual. In this realm, you have your will, intellect, and emotions. Your soul is the signature of yourself. Also, the soul works as a middle man between the spirit man to interpret that information that is received from the spiritual realm in a way so you can understand it and pass along to your brain and body. Your spirit man is the part that is conscious of God himself. It is in the realm that we commune and fellowship with God and realms of the spirit. We need our spirit man to be born again so we can worship God who is a spirit in the spiritual realm and in truth.

Scientists have found out through their research recently that the part of the body that has the most thinking activity is actually the heart. Any area of the body that is doing thinking and communicating is signified by neurons. By the presence of neurons, scientists have a key to what areas are thinking. Neurons surprisingly, are in great numbers in the brain, gut, and the heart. And the heart contains the most neurons. It is through the neurons that signals are sent through the body and the heart, brain, and the gut are talking to each other. This is why we say we can feel in our gut because our gut is the mind of the soulish realm and gives us a certain intuition that makes an impression on our emotions. As said earlier, the spirit, soul, and body communicate with one another to process information gained from each realm. The key is to get all parts of us in alignment with each other. The goal is to tap into the life of the Spirit, and let it flow through our soul, so it can impact the physical realm around us. The heart is the mind , thinking center, and storage aspect of our spirit man.

Luke 6 (KJV)

45 A good man out of the good treasure of his heart bringeth forth that which is

101

good; and an evil man out of the evil treasure of his heart bringeth forth that which is evil: for of the abundance of the heart his mouth speaketh.

I was always taught there was an order to things when it comes to manifesting things in our lives. I was told to "Watch your thoughts, because it becomes words. Watch your words because they become actions. Watch your actions because that is what shapes your world around you." So if we now know that our thoughts are originating to our heart in the spiritual realm, then it makes sense that the bible says that out of the abundance of your heart, the mouth speaks. If your heart has thoughts then eventually you are going to believe those thoughts and begin to speak it. And we know that life and death is in the power of the tongue. The key is what is our heart connected and fueled by. Is it connected to evil or good? Is it renewed and connected to God or is it dead in darkness? A good man as in the above passage brings good treasure out of his heart but an evil man brings evil treasure out of his heart. Another scripture lets us know that we have this treasure hidden in earthen vessels. That treasure that God intends is for us to birth and live what is on our destiny scrolls housed in our heart. We are called to be a peculiar treasure in God's sight. As a man thinks (in his heart), so is he.

Why Circumcision?

Romans 2 (KJV)
28 For he is not a Jew, which is one outwardly; neither is that circumcision, which is outward in the flesh:
*29 But he is a Jew, **which is one inwardly; and circumcision is that of the heart, in the spirit**, and not in the letter; whose praise is not of men, but of God.*

Circumcision is the removal of the flesh of the foreskin of the male penis. This was instituted by God with Abraham and his seed in the natural world as a sign of covenant. He was to circumcise his whole house even his manservants no matter what age they were. Even from this moment, Abram's name was changed to Abraham and his destiny as father of many nations was pronounced over him. From then on, any male child that was born was circumcised and officially named on the 8th day. So even though the male child was born one way when it came to his reproductive organ, then on the 8th day flesh was removed and now he looks different down there. The number 8 represents a new beginning. Also, on that day he received a name which represents identity and purpose for names representing the nature of a person and was prophetic concerning their destiny. You did not just pick some random name. It was chosen for a specific reason. So this is part of that process in the natural realm but as you can already see, it has many spiritual symbolisms. God uses the things in the natural at times to point to the spiritual. Like even in the physical, there is male and female, but God spiritually is talking to all of us from a perspective that he has called us to be sons of the kingdom of God. The covenants of the Old Testament were shadows and types to point to what God wanted to establish in the new covenant. In the new covenant, it was more about the inner than the outward. It was more about the spiritual than the physical. It was more about the nature of the heart instead of just good works. It was about one new man instead of just about one bloodline in the earth. Christ was the savior of the whole world.

Some people get caught up in genealogies and bloodlines. Some are saying we are Jews because we carry the physical bloodline of Abraham, Isaac, and Jacob. And I believe that the physical Israel has certain promises that God will fulfill in the end times. But through the new covenant, it is not about if you are circumcised in the flesh but rather are you circumcised in your heart. This is the person who is a Jew inwardly and has a covenant with the Almighty God. All have been made one in the spirit by the cross of Jesus Christ. So this is why we need circumcision of the heart because it is a sign of covenant with the Master. If our heart is not circumcised, we can not produce and manifest the life of God that he has ordained for us. This is not a new concept after the cross of Christ. It was God's initial intention even with Abraham that the physical circumcision was to be parallel to the inner circumcision. You see scriptures to the children of Israel calling for them to have their hearts circumcised. He is calling for something deeper within.

In a previous chapter, we discussed that the first cell of a fetus after the sperm meets the egg contains the scroll of destiny from eternity and the spark of life. But also, later it is used in conjunction with the other cells formed to create the heart first. The heart is the first organ created in the womb wrapping around the scroll of destiny. But then the other cells that carry the testimony of our flesh began to cover that initial cell and the heart. The testimony of the Most High placed in us is now hidden and must not be uncovered by removing the nature of the flesh within the heart so that we can walk as God has ordained for to walk. Circumcision of the heart is vital and key to occur in our spiritual journey so we can be all we can be in the army of the Lord.

Removal of the Foreskin

Hebrews 4 (KJV)
*12 For the **word of God is quick, and powerful, and sharper than any twoedged sword**, piercing even to the **dividing asunder of soul and spirit**, and of the joints and marrow, and is a **discerner of the thoughts and intents of the heart**.*

The foreskin over our heart represents the flesh nature. During circumcision in the natural realm , usually a knife or some other sharp object is utilized to remove the foreskin. It is the same way in the heart. The Word, Christ in you, which is the sword of the Spirit, must begin to circumcise the flesh nature from the heart. It is the sword of the Spirit which means it only can cut that which is spiritual. The sword is so precise that it even cuts asunder that which is soulish versus that which is spiritual. This sword, the Word of God, removes things so now we can discern and see truly what is the intents and thoughts of the heart. (There is another scripture showing you that the heart thinks.) We can begin to discern what God is saying in our heart concerning us. We need heart surgery so that we can walk according to the beat and rhythm of God and heaven.

In Hebrews 10, we are shown that Christ came to remove another aspect that is hindering us. When Christ died on the cross the veil that led to the Holy of Holies was ripped into two. This veil it lets you know represents the flesh. Here in the temple Christ removed the flesh within the physical temple. We are the temple of God in the earth and in us he is removing the flesh nature that limits us from entering into the Holy of Holies within us. There is a place in us that we should have sweet communion with God where his will is revealed and grace is released so we can carry out his will and our destiny.The veil has been taken away so that we can now walk boldly into the throne room of God so we can receive grace in our time of need. Christ is in us and he is sitting on the throne of our heart. If we yield to him, he will remove the veil in our heart so we can be free and have liberty to fellowship with the Master and be led by him. In the 3rd chapter of 2nd Corinthians, we know that the Lord is that Spirit in us that removes the veil and where the Lord is, there is liberty. How do you begin the process of removing the flesh and letting circumcision occur in your heart? You turn to the Lord within and let him change and transform you from the inside out. By removing the veil you will have access to the testimony scrolls of destiny inside you.

Other Benefits of Circumcision

As there are benefits naturally when it comes to circumcision, there are also benefits that we can enjoy from a spiritual perspective when the Master performs this holy operation in our heart. In the natural world, the penis appearance is changed from the way it was when the male child was born. So this shows that circumcision of our heart changes the way we look. We are born again and now we are a new creation. Also, it removes the covering and foreskin, which means that the part of us that is self is removed. Sometimes we have aspirations and plans that we have builded up in our minds concerning our lives but it was not the will of God. We need to die to those fantasies and dreams. Circumcision of the heart does that for us. Men know that from being circumcised that the penis around the head area is now more sensitive to touch. Through the sword of the Spirit and the Word of God, we are now more sensitive to the Most High God. Also, with the foreskin removed it is easier now to clean the head of the penis. Once Christ removes certain things from our heart, it is now easy to clean. Oh how our heart should cry to God to say "Give me a clean heart". Now with the foreskin removed, the water of the washing of the Word can come in and clean more efficiently the things in our heart.

The benefits of the hand of Christ operating in our heart are endless. When your spirit man is born again by your confession to Christ, your spirit man is male. I will release a mystery. The heart which is the mind of the spirit, is the penis or the reproductive center that contains the seeds that will be released to birth things in the physical realm. The foreskin and all flesh natured remnants must be removed. Your soul is more so feminine as it is what houses the emotions and things like that. It is the goal for your renewed spirit to lead to the renewal of your soul so that your soul now can become the bride of Christ and the spirit that was first cut asunder by the Sword of the Spirit can now be rejoined in holy matrimony and oneness. The spirit man that is masculine as it matures becomes the part that is called to be conformed to the image of the Son and called to sonship. This is the goal that through circumcision of the heart you can become a mature son of God who walks in his full destiny and causes your soul and body to come in alignment with the kingdom of God. The soul the wife/bride will submit to the spirit man (husband) that is joined to Christ. This is all so you are changed and

Christ can be fully formed in you. When the male child is circumcised on the 8th day, he is named. When your stony flesh nature cover is removed from your heart, you have a new name. This new name speaks of the destiny and scroll that was connected to you from eternity. Your heart is now seeded with a new nature ready to do the will of God.

Intimacy With The True Head

Deuteronomy 30 (KJV)
*6 And the Lord thy God will **circumcise thine heart**, and the heart of thy seed, to love the Lord thy God with all thine heart, and with all thy soul, that thou mayest live.*

The aforementioned scripture of Romans 8:27 speaks to us searching the heart to know the mind of the Spirit and the will of God. The testimony scroll of God that contains his will and destiny for our lives is in our heart. He wants us to seek with everything that is available so we can return to that which is in a sense a bread crumb trail to lead you back to that which is eternal. That is the Most High God. From the above passage, we know that it is the Most High himself who will circumcise our heart. The goal of being in the new covenant which circumcision is a sign of is for God to be the true head in your life where in him we live, move, and have our being in Him. Just like with a body that has a head and in that head is a brain and it sends signals to the body so the body can follow the lead of the head. In this journey, the Christ in you wants to use his sword to remove all that is earthly and fleshly to reveal his will for you. He also wants to etch in your heart his laws and commandments and change your nature so he which is the true head can come forth and shine in your life.

That is what circumcision is about revealing that true head that was hidden. Christ in us, the hope of glory, is the true head. The aim is to have intimacy with him. The above passage not only points to who will be circumcising but it also shows that the effect of circumcision is to align our heart and nature so we can freely love the Lord with all our heart and soul. By loving him with all our heart and soul, it will cause us to live the way God intended by his eternal will and testimony that he had originally proclaimed over us before we were in our mother's womb. The removal of the veil, the obstacles and distractions of the earth brings us to a place where we can be naked before the Lord and the Lord himself, be in a sense, exposed and unveiled as well. We can enjoy one another freely and his life and seed can penetrate our life and birth destiny and purpose in us. This intimacy must be fueled by love and not where we are made like a robot to serve him. Our heart must be in the right posture and nature so that we can love him with true adoration. This is why circumcision of the heart is needed so much. It removes the blinders so love can fuel our obedience to him and he can be the true head and king over our lives.

The Garden That Produces Fruit

The spirit or man when re-birthed is joined to the Lord and is the husband awaiting to be one with the bride (the soul) within man. The term "husband" is actually a term that is linked to agriculture and farming. It was the husbandman who cared for and oversaw the garden. It was the husbandman who began to plant seed and make sure that the right type of growth was happening in the garden. When God placed man in the garden, his job was to be a husbandman in the garden to guard and keep it. In mankind, is the garden of the heart. The heart is a garden waiting for the right seeds to be planted so it can create a harvest to take to market so the soul can be fed from what has been produced in the garden of the heart. The heart is a part of the spirit that produces fruit. That is why the term for walking in faith, love, temperance, goodness is the fruit of the Spirit. The fruit is produced in the garden of the heart with the right seeds and the watering of the Holy Spirit.

The right seeds produce the fruit of the Spirit, but the wrong seeds eventually lead to the manifestation of the works of the flesh. That which is born of spirit is spirit and that which is born of flesh is flesh. The seeds that must be planted are the seeds that are in the storehouse of our testimony scrolls of destiny hidden in our heart. The storehouse must be opened and revealed so the seeds off the page of the scroll of destiny can then be planted and watered. Sometimes, while we were sleeping and not paying attention, the enemy planted seeds in us and there was a mixture of wheat and tares in us. It is the process of circumcision that goes through the garden and removes the tares and prunes the garden so that the true fruit of our destiny can come forth. If this does not happen the tares and thorns will choke the word of destiny in our heart. We need the operation of Jesus Christ in us and the Holy Spirit together to work in unison to cause us to walk according to the seeds of the scroll of destiny in our heart. From there, the thoughts of our heart (seeds) can be his thoughts and the harvest in our heart can flow to our soul and to our body and to those around us.

Prayer

Heavenly Father above, I come to you in the name of Jesus Christ and I ask that you do heart surgery on everyone who reads this book. May the sword of the Spirit pierce their hearts and begin to remove everything that is not like you. May all the influences of the world and other sources be cut away so that the true head of Christ be revealed. Lead them to begin to know what is on the scroll of destiny in their heart. Give them a clean heart that begins to produce the correct fruit in their lives. Give them a new name in the spirit which is the name that you named them from the beginning. Change their nature to glorify you. May they be more sensitive to the leading of the Holy Spirit. Open up the eyes of their heart by removing the scales and foreskin so they can see the scroll of destiny. May the garden of their heart be planted with the right seeds and watered by the Holy Spirit. I thank you in advance for your operation in their inner man. Amen.

Chapter 9 : PRAYER & FASTING

* * *

Fulfilling our destiny for the sake of our King should be one of our top priorities. We need work of the Holy Spirit and Christ operating within to bring us to a place of unveiling the scroll of destiny. We need to know what is on the scroll that he has written concerning all our members before the foundation of the world. Our heart must be pure to see what God wants of us and from there, desire with all our being his will for us. Once we have that knowledge, we use that knowledge to move forward in faith and all diligence to perform it. We need to use all the tools that the Father has given us to walk in our full identity. We need prayer and fasting in our life to make us more complete.

Your Full Potential

Matthew 10 (KJV)
*1 And when he had called unto him his twelve disciples, he gave them **power** against **unclean spirits**, to cast them out, and to heal **all manner of sickness** and **all manner of disease.***

Matthew 17 (KJV)

18 And Jesus rebuked the devil; and he departed out of him: and the child was cured from that very hour.

*19 Then came the disciples to Jesus apart, and said, **Why could not we cast him out?***

20 And Jesus said unto them, Because of your unbelief: for verily I say unto you, If ye have faith as a grain of mustard seed, ye shall say unto this mountain, Remove hence to yonder place; and it shall remove; and nothing shall be impossible unto you.

*21 Howbeit **this kind goeth not out but by prayer and fasting.***

The Father is looking for us to be more complete in him and walk in his fullness. You might be wondering why I selected this above two groupings of scriptures. It is because they are highly connected and relate to one another. In the first passage of Matthew 10, we see a scene where the Lord Jesus called his twelve disciples and he ordained them and gave them power over all unclean spirits and all sickness. Another way we can say this is that it was proclaimed over them that they had access to the power of God a certain way so they can fulfill a certain purpose and destiny that was authorized by Christ himself. And this is a sense every man and woman in the world that before the foundation of the world, there were some things that was spoken over you and released over your life your you to walk in but for some reason some of us find it hard to walk in the full potential of what sits on our life even though we know we have been called to certain things.

Why is this so? It is because there are certain things that we are not doing to activate the full realm of who we are. Scientists say that we have this brain that has all this potential and power but most human beings are only using a small portion of it. And this dilemma that we sometimes fall in. We know we have been called to certain things. We can sense the power there to perform a thing but when it is time to step to the plate, we only get partial or no results. Part of the secret is that prayer and fasting is a super one-two combo punch to catapult you in the high stratosphere of your identity. In the passage of

Matthew 17, we see later the same disciples who were empowered to cast out demons and heal all sickness in a position where there is a demonic spirit that none of them could cast out. Twelve were anointed and ordained to walk in this but none of the twelve could do it. They bring the person to Jesus and he casts the spirit out right away. You probably are saying that we are talking about Jesus Christ the Messiah and that is why he was able to perform the act. . But that was not Jesus' stance. His stance was not that I am better than you. His lesson on why they could not do it was that they need to utilize prayer and fasting to unlock their full potential. Jesus' message was actually you will do greater works.

Prayer is so important in revealing our destiny to us but also empowering us to walk in our destiny. Fasting works in conjunction to shape and humble us so we can yield to the leading of the Holy Spirit. Some of us might know our purpose but we are stuck because of our prayer and fasting life. Some might not have a clue at all and clarity is not going to come to walk in prayer and fasting at another level. I am surprised at how many times how many people who have been walking with the Lord for years but have never fasted before. A lot of times in the midst of counseling and ministry sessions with people, the simple answer is that they need to engage in prayer and fasting. We are in the microwave and fast food generation where we want this our way , right away. But God is saying I need you to trust the process and seek me with prayer and fasting so I can bring you to your full potential. To find and unravel the scroll of destiny in you and for you to actually fulfill that destiny, prayer and fasting must be a lifestyle for you.

Prayer Manifests the Testimony of God

Prayer in simple terms is communication with God. This is not in one direction but is a two way conversation. A lot of times people approach prayer with just us talking to God and not really expecting to hear back from him. Or the other issue might be that we only give him a quick five minutes to say some words to him and never take time to wait and listen to what he will say back or reveal to us. The mindset of prayer should be that it is a conversation and fellowship with the Most High and heaven. The focus of this book is around the scroll of destiny and we will not be able to go into the deep depths of the processes of prayer. But if you want to look at a guide on how to pray, the Lord Jesus in Matthew 6.

Matthew 6 (KJV)

8 Be not ye therefore like unto them: for your Father knoweth what things ye have need of, before ye ask him.

9 After this manner therefore pray ye: Our Father which art in heaven, Hallowed be thy name.

10 Thy kingdom come, Thy will be done in earth, as it is in heaven.

11 Give us this day our daily bread.

12 And forgive us our debts, as we forgive our debtors.

13 And lead us not into temptation, but deliver us from evil: For thine is the kingdom, and the power, and the glory, for ever. Amen.

There are some who use this prayer and say it verbatim. And there is not anything wrong with that. But I believe the Messiah was showing us a pattern on how to pray. He starts off in verse 9 by saying "after this manner" we should pray. It is a pattern. It is a guideline on how to pray. You first start off with thanksgiving , praise, and acknowledging him as your Father and King. And there are aspects of asking for his daily bread which is spiritual and asking for forgiveness. Also, you ask for protection against the enemy. The key is not asking for things because in verse 8, he says that the Father knows what you are already in need of. So if the Father already knows what we are in need of, then why are we praying. We are praying so that the Father can reveal something to us that is greater than our earthly needs on the earth. He wants to reveal who we are and why we are here. The best person to receive that information from is the one who created you. It is something about a father or mother, speaking over their child's life concerning who they are by shaping them with their words. Sometimes in the natural world, that shaping is bad because parents are saying the wrong thing. But when we come to our heavenly Father to get to a place to fellowship with him and hear what he has to say, the words he speaks will be spirit and life and exactly what is needed at that moment.

When we talk about the word "testimony", it is that person recounting activities from their perspective. Through prayer we receive the testimony of God of his will that he has for us. We are placed in a position to see or hear the contents of the scroll within us be communicated to us. As his will is made known we then continually come to prayer with a mindset to speak his will and declare it so that it can manifest in our life. Life and death is in the power of the tongue. When you are in the know and you know that you know, then by faith you can release his Word and his will through prayer to manifest his testimony in your life.

The flow of prayer is to manifest God's will and that which is already ordained in heaven on earth. In verse 10, its focus is that we are praying that God's will be done and that what manifests on earth lines up with what heaven's testimony is. Our heavenly Father is also a king and the earth is also his domain. Prayer is the vehicle to align with the king's decree out of heaven and release it into the earth. That is why our prayer should be to let his kingdom , his reign, and his will come into the earth and our lives. And even the ending part of the prayer is the kingdom, power, and glory is his. Our goal of prayer is to tap into his kingdom, his power, and glory so that it can fuel us to fulfill our destiny. The kingdom of God in us is the domain that he has called to rule and reign in. The kingdom of God in us speaks to our destiny and that which was uniquely designed and ordained just for us. The power of God is the power that gives us backing and fueling to do what he has called us to do. The power helps us to enforce the rule and keep order in our domain in life. The glory of God is the weight, the fullness, and abundance that manifest in our lives when we are positioned to where God

115

has called us. It is the glory that we walk in when we use the power of God available to overcome the enemy and sit in the victor's chair with dominion and the spoils of war. It is to walk in the fullness of everything that God is and has in store for our lives. We only tap into the kingdom, the power, and glory assigned to us through prayer.

The aim of prayer is to manifest God's intention and testimony of the before in our lives. We need to believe this during prayer so that at the end we can proclaim with faith "Amen" which means "So be it". It is a setup. Things were set up for us in the heavenly places and set up within us and prayer is the vehicle in which we pull the heavenly things down and the inward things out of our being. Prayer brings manifestation of that which is eternal in your life. Once we know through prayer what his will is, then we can be assured that when we release his will and word through our mouth, that his Word will not return back to him empty and void. But it will accomplish that which it was sent to do.

Meditating the Word

We are still in the realm of prayer and it might seem strange to have a heading of "Meditating the Word". How does that align with prayer? The target of prayer is to pray the will of God which is his Word. When you can't necessarily hear yet through his spoken rhema word, then you need to turn to the written word to know what his will is. A little secret is that as you meditate on the written Word, it activates a part in you to hear the spoken word with clarity and have the ability to discern the voice of God in you. Notice, I did not say read the bible. I am encouraging you to not just read or memorize the Word but to meditate the Word. This is a very important aspect of prayer.

Without going into much detail, we can look at the pattern of the tabernacle and temple in scripture, and see the pattern of prayer. You enter in with thanksgiving, praise, and a sacrifice. Then there is another section called the Holy Place that then can eventually lead you to the Holy of Holies where the voice of God and the glory of God dwells. This of course, is the end game we want to reach during prayer. I want to point our attention to the middle section (The Holy Place). In it is a candlestick, altar of incense, and a table of showbread. It is interesting that with part of the Lord's prayer, we are asking the Father to give us our daily bread. This bread represents the word of God that we should be feasting on. Prayer should be changing and transforming us in some ways. It should also refresh us, feed us, and nourish us. Part of this comes from the bread of life contained in his Word. We are not to go past this part of the room quickly. We need to meditate the Word of God.

We are to pray his Word and his will but what does meditating the Word do for us. This is the part that causes our soul, mind, and heart to align with the will and nature of God. What is meditation? It means from a biblical position, not to go somewhere and get still and bring nothingness in your mind. But it means to ponder and speak to oneself. I like to liken meditation of the Word to slowly eating something so you can taste all the flavor of the food item and also that you can chew it thoroughly so it can digest properly. We are not to take big chunks at one time or else we can choke as well. To start off, take a scripture that you might want deeper revelation of or you want the essence of that scripture to become you. Then you began to take that scripture and say it out loud over and over again till you began to receive more revelation by the Holy Spirit concerning that scripture. Sometimes it is not about you getting revelation about the scripture but the essence and nature of that scripture filling you up and changing the inner nature of you to empower you for something. This is an important part of prayer that causes you to change you inwardly to allow you to manifest his will and Word in you and around you.

Communication With Heaven

2 Chronicles 7 (KJV)
*14 If my people, which are **called by my name**, shall **humble themselves**, and*
pray, and seek my face**, and turn from their wicked ways; **then will I hear
***from heaven**, and will forgive their sin, and will heal their land.*

Prayer and fasting allows you to come to a place where you communicate with heaven. It enables a signal and frequency where both parties can tune in so there can be a receiving and transmitting of information. In the context of the above passage, God is saying if his people do certain things, then he will eventually heal the land. The goal is to bring the fullness of his will (destiny) to manifest in the earth. Here the people were the children of Israel from a physical perspective but now in the new covenant where he has made one new man, we are his people who trust in Christ and know that their beginning was eternal. Those who begin to realize that we are called by his name from eternity and we were in the Father. We will talk about this more later, but "humble themselves" here means fasting. It is the combination of prayer and fasting with the intent of seeking his face that causes communication in heaven. When we pray and fast, a signal ascends in the heavens. Why does it ascend? It ascends because we spiritually originate from the heavens but also, when our words align with the substance and will of God, it allows access to rise to a place that it can be heard before God. The angels lift our words because their job is to hasten to perform his Word.

Our words are not just to be raised to a place where God can hear from heaven but it is his pleasure to be able to transmit back to us a message. That message might be healing, forgiveness, things concerning your destiny, and so on. But the point there is a channel way that is setup so we can communicate with our Heaven Father. That is where the prayer begins.

"Our Heavenly Father". That is the direction of prayer to reach our heavenly Father. The Holy Spirit makes intercession for us according to the will of God to the Heavenly Father. Jesus Christ even at the right hand of the Father makes intercession for us to the Heavenly Father. This is the pattern that we should take note of. Our hope should be to communicate with heaven through prayer. I use the general term "Heaven" because this points to the Father, Jesus, the Holy Spirit, and sometimes his angels. The Father did not place us on the earth just to fend for ourselves. But he has assembled a team who is cheering you on and there for help when we need it so we can eventually be the praise of his glory in the earth.

Sometimes the two way communication does not happen quickly. Sometimes through prayer we have to wait for his reply. Daniel the prophet one time had to pray and fast for 21 days before an angel showed up with an answer. It is not that the angel decided to come 21 days later but actually the angel was dispatched as soon as the first prayer on the first day was released but due to spiritual warfare, it took a while to get the answer. We have to understand we are in a war with the enemy and our flesh and sometimes it takes time for us to get the message. The key is being patient and persistent to receive the message and also what you do with the message when you receive it. Of course sometimes the Master gives us instructions and directions that calls for our surrender and obedience. The issue is sometimes things are not one day projects but can be one month, one year, ten year, 30 year projects. In other words, sometimes the process of manifesting that from heaven into the earth takes time depending on the situation. That is why one of the fruits of the spirit is patience.

Because sometimes in the earth realm, it takes time and our physical brain is finite, we have to be intentional to write some things down and record it some type of way. With prayer, you must have a journal or recording device around so you can capture the crumbs from heaven. When it comes to things of our destiny scroll , it does not always happen where, all of sudden you ask God to reveal the scroll and an angel appears right there with a scroll and you see the whole contents at one time. I wish it worked like that. But the truth is that our God is a line upon line, and precept upon precept type of God. He releases things in stages. If he gave the whole package at once we might not be ready for it all at once or destroy the package because we don't understand the order of things. He is a God of order and protocol. Sometimes in our sessions of prayer and communication of God, we might get glimpses or pieces. When this happens we need to write it down or capture it some way so we can later come and grab the puzzle piece when another puzzle piece comes. Eventually over time we will have a fuller picture of what he is calling us to so we can walk it out.

One time around 2008, I was seeking the Lord to reveal more to me about my destiny and to show me the whole picture because I wanted to know more. During that time in prayer, I had a vision. At the time I had a one year old son, and in the vision I saw my son in a highchair in the kitchen. And there was a plate of food on the top of the highchair. He did not eat all the food but he was signaling in a kids way by banging on the table part and saying "More", that he wanted more food. In the vision, I say to my son, "You have to finish what is on your plate first before I give you more food". I then came out the vision and I knew instantly in my spirit what the Lord was saying to me. I thought it was ironic and funny that he would use a scene of me talking to my son for him to speak a message to his son (me). It is not always going to come in one big total put together package. It will come in pieces. When it comes in pieces, write the vision down so when it is time you can run with the vision. But also, do all that you can do with the pieces you have, so he can release more pieces of that scroll to you. Keep the communication open with heaven so you can get all the chapters of the book (scroll) of life that he has written concerning you.

Accessing the Mysteries of Your Destiny

1 Corinthians 14 (KJV)
*2 For he that **speaketh in an unknown tongue speaketh not unto men**, but unto God: for no man understandeth him; **howbeit in the spirit he speaketh mysteries**.*

*4 He that **speaketh in an unknown tongue edifieth himself**; but he that prophesieth edifieth the church.*

The things of the heavens and the spirit to the natural mind are mysteries and have to be spiritually discerned. One of the ways to begin to crack the code to begin to see and know the mysteries is through tongues. I know some might be against tongues but I can't deny that it takes things to a higher level. Tongues tune your spirit man to align to the frequency of God so you can receive more from him. If you have not been baptized with the Holy Spirit where you speak in tongues your heavenly language, then just ask him in faith expecting to receive. In verse 4 above it says that if a person speaks in tongues then he edifies himself. That word edify in the Greek means to to lift up above and charge like how you will charge a battery for power. Tongues enable you to be lifted up above your natural self but it also fills your spirit man with power. That is why in Acts 1:8, we know that after that the Holy Ghost comes upon you, you shall receive power. We need that power so we can walk into the fullness of our destiny.

Speaking in tongues is not initially for you because it is not to other men and women per se but it is for you to build up so you can be a source of blessing to others. I was probably about thirteen or fourteen when I was baptized with the Holy Ghost with the evidence of speaking in tongues. From my Pentecostal background at the time, my understanding was that the tongues came out only when you praised God or something. That was all I observed at the time. But I had some friends that I would hang out with all the time like brothers. They were into watching a lot of TBN (Christian television) and loved to watch Benny Hinn who I did not know much about. One day we were talking about prayer and they let me know that there were different levels of prayer and began to list them. The last one they listed was the level of "praying in tongues". The words hit me like a ton of bricks. I had never heard that before and it created a longing in me. So that very night I went home and began to pray in tongues. At first, I would just say a syllable here and there while praising God, but taking the approach of praying in tongues, it began to blossom in a full blown language. I realized that it perked my spirit up to receive the mysteries of God. What type of mysteries? Mysteries of the spiritual realm, the Word of God, and your destiny began to open up before me and bring me into a different dimension of power and knowing.

1 Corinthians 14 (KJV)
*14 For if **I pray in an unknown tongue, my spirit prayeth**, but my understanding is unfruitful.*
*15 What is it then? **I will pray with the spirit, and I will pray with the understanding also: I will sing with the spirit, and I will sing with the understanding also.***

The mysteries of God through tongues do not all come at one time. It is like you begin to release the mysteries through tongues and it activates your spirit man, and then as you continue, your spirit man begins to interpret and drop translations to your soul so that you can comprehend with a certain understanding. When you first begin to speak in tongues, you don't have a clue what is being said. To be honest, your natural mind is going to reject it and say to stop this foolishness. But our God uses the foolish things of the world to confound the wise. As long as you are trying to comprehend it naturally, you will never get to the place of revelation of the mysteries by the Spirit. So you must press pass the doubts and fears of the natural mind.

You must ask the Holy Spirit for the interpretation. As in the above passage, when you speak in tongues, it is your spirit man praying as it taps into the spiritual realm and speaks its mysteries. That is one frequency and level that the natural mind can't initially understand. That is why verse 15 shows us the pattern, you begin in the spirit and you end in the natural understanding. You pray in the spirit through tongues and then you speak with an understanding of the mysteries. You sing in the spirit through tongues and then you sing with understanding the mysteries. One again as the mysteries are being revealed, try your best when you can to capture the mysteries.

Jude (KJV)

20 But ye, beloved, building up yourselves on your most holy faith, praying in the Holy Ghost,

The above passage reiterates that through praying in the Holy Ghost by tongues we are building ourselves up. But it goes deeper and shows up that we build ourselves upon the foundation of faith. When you look in the Greek when it comes to building in this verse, it points to building a superstructure above something else that is a foundation. The foundation is faith. Why is this important to see this way? It is because faith is the substance of things hoped for which is our destiny. It is because faith is the evidence and testimony of things unseen which is our destiny. It is because God has dealt to every man the measure of faith in our mother womb that pertains to our destiny. The scroll of faith is within us and Jesus is the author of that scroll of faith and also the finisher of it. Tongues cause you to build on the foundation of the scroll of destiny and build faith in you so the mysteries concerning things you hope for can be revealed to you. This reveals other pieces of the blueprint on how we should build ourselves and life according to the plans of the Master. I can't say it any other way. Tongues are a vital part of prayer that reveals the mysteries of God and pieces of the testimony scrolls of destiny within us.

Fasting Weakens The Voice of the Enemy

Isaiah 58 (KJV)

*5 Is it such a fast that I have chosen? a day for a **man to afflict his soul**? is it to bow down his head as a bulrush, and to spread sackcloth and ashes under him? wilt thou call this a fast, and an acceptable day to the Lord?*
*6 Is not this the fast that I have chosen? **to loose the bands of wickedness**, to **undo the heavy burdens**, and to **let the oppressed go free**, and that ye **break every yoke**?*
*7 Is it not to deal thy bread to the hungry, and that thou bring the poor that are cast out to thy house? when thou seest the naked, **that thou cover him; and that thou hide not thyself from thine own flesh**?*
*8 Then shall **thy light break forth as the morning**, and thine health shall spring forth speedily: and **thy righteousness shall go before thee; the glory of the Lord shall be thy reward**.*

What is fasting? Someone might say that fasting is a form of denying yourself by limiting your food and drink intake for a period of time. This is true on some level but there is more. Anyone can not eat or drink for a period of time but the question is what are you doing during the time that you are not eating? Are you still watching a lot of television, having a whole lot of conversation with idle words, looking constantly on Facebook and Instagram, or doing normal activities? This should not be the activities that go along with fasting. With fasting our mindset should be seeking the Lord and not only putting away food but also putting away all the other distractions and busyness of the day. Also, then mixing with prayer and reading of the Word. This should be the mindset and process when it comes to fasting.

You might think, how long should I fast for? Well it depends on how long you are being led to fast? What are you trying to attain with your fast? (Your fast should have intentional expectations) How long are you willing to go to reach your goal? You might have thought you were going to fast for a day but you needed to press longer to reach the goal you were looking for. Sometimes you might fast for a certain time period of the day like 6am to 6pm with no water or food. There are times you might do a whole day. Some might do 3 days of fasting even at times with no food or water. But I recommend that if you go above 3 days, then you should incorporate water. Some might just do it for a period of time, only juice or no meat at all. It might not be food that you are letting go of. It might be that you need to step away from television and social media and certain types of music for a period of time and use that time to seek the Lord. Fasting comes in many ways and formats.

So that covered more of a textbook definition of what fasting is, but now let's look at what is happening in the spiritual and inner man during fasting. In verse 5 above, we are told that fasting afflicts the soul. What does that mean? The soul is the part of you that makes you unique with being the seat of the emotions, will, and intellect. Sometimes the testimony of the flesh is influencing the aspect of your emotions, will and reasoning. Your emotions might be out of whack and causing you to be out of the will and rest of God. Sometimes your will is siding with disobedience rather than to the things of God and your destiny. There might be an aspect that your intellect and reasoning is looking more at what is seen in the natural and the limitations of the physical realm and not believing in the promises of God. In the soul, the voice of the testimony of the flesh and the will of the enemy might be strong and present. This is where fasting comes in. It afflicts and beats in submission the soul to align with the voice of your spirit man that is one with the Holy Spirit. Even witches and those of the occult fast often to make them more sharper in the spiritual realm. But in their case, their spirit man is not renewed and connected to demonic forces. Nevertheless, they understand it as a vital spiritual exercise for power. Fasting weakens the influence of the enemy and causes you to walk in your full potential as God seems fit. It causes you to decrease, so he can increase in you.

In verses 6 through 8 of Isaiah 58 which I called the fasting chapter, it outlines the other benefits of fasting. One of the first benefits of afflicting the soul is that the bands of wickedness and the flesh nature is loosened. Fasting causes the hold and grip of nature of the flesh to be broken off your life. Another benefit is that the heaven burdens within you like the sins and the weights that weigh you down are lifted off your life through fasting. Fasting causes those who are oppressed by the enemy to be set free. If the enemy and the testimony of the enemy presses down the God intended you down, fasting causes that stronghold to be broken. The yoke of bondage will be removed through fasting. The aspect about yokes is that they are used to be placed around your neck so that the person who holds the yoke can control the direction you go in. Some of us have been in places where the yoke of the enemy was leading us to do all types of things. But it is through the process of fasting that the yoke of the enemy will be removed and the yoke of Christ whose burden is light can be the replacement. When this happens, then we can be guided by Christ into the destiny that we are called into.

Verse 7 shows us that nakedness will be covered. When we are naked our flesh is showing. Fasting covers and gets rid of the flesh nature so we can be covered with the robe of righteousness. When this happens the darkness that is being displayed by the enemy is then scattered and fasting causes the light of God to shine within us as alluded to in verse 8. Some of us have been in darkness and gloom and it was one big nightmare but fasting will cause light to shine as in the morning. Fasting will bring a new dawning and day into your life. And from there righteousness can shine forth in our life which is having right standing before the Father. To be in right standing you have to walk in Him, his ways, and your destiny. The end result will be the glory of God in your life. The glory is the weight and abundance of the Father being released in your life. The glory is the manifestation of the fullness of who he is all and all that he intended in your life. Fasting leads you to a place where the enemy is dethroned in your life and the King of glory is reigning in your life so you can walk according to the decree of the true King.

Grace To the Humble

Psalms 35 (KJV)

13 But as for me, when they were sick, my clothing was sackcloth: **I humbled my soul with fasting***; and my prayer returned into mine own bosom.*

James 4 (KJV)

6 But he giveth more grace. Wherefore he saith, **God resisteth the proud, but giveth grace unto the humble.**

Another aspect of fasting that I hinted to earlier is that fasting humbles you. It puts you in a place of submission and humility. It causes the parts in you that are not aligned with God to go under and aligns your will and emotions in full surrender to the King of glory. In Psalms 35:13, King David lets us know that he humbled his soul by fasting and it worked in conjunction with his prayer that his answer to his prayer returned to him. Fasting caused the return communication of God and heaven to transmit and answer and reply to the bosom and inner man of David. Oh the glory that is released through fasting to impact your prayers. There is a principle in the word of God that he rewards those who humble themselves before him. One of the things that God hates is pride and fasting deals with pride. Pride causes you to be rejected by God, but humbling yourself through things like prayer, fasting, and worship, it draws you to a secret place with God.

James 4:6, lets us know that God gives grace to the humble. What is grace? It is the supernatural endowment of God in you to empower you to do the will of God and your destiny. When we fast and humble ourselves before the Lord, it brings us into position to receive a deposit within us. That deposit contains the grace of God. It contains the power of God. It contains the ability of God. It contains the embedded code of instruction for you that aligns you to your destiny. Grace is given through fasting to cause you to be able to peek into the testimony scroll of destiny that the Father has granted to you with your name on it. The humbling of your soul through fasting brings you to the posture of surrender and the King of glory rewards this posture with his grace, power, and nuggets of destiny.

Mixture & The War

The premise of this book is that we are in a war. The enemy is against us becoming overcomers. But in the book of Revelation we are told that we overcome the enemy by the blood of the Lamb and the Word of our testimony. That testimony is from the beginning and deals with our destiny aligning with the testimony of the Father and Christ that they had concerning us before the foundation of the Word. When we were placed in our mother's womb that testimony scroll was placed in our heart but unfortunately because of the fall of man, another testimony of our flesh which was planted by the enemy began to try to smother the testimony of the Lord. So hence, there is a war within us on which testimony can vibrate and make the most noise in our lives. There is a principle I see in the business world and also even when it comes to home life. The thing that makes the most noise in most cases is what is going to get the most attention. In business, the customer who makes the most noise is the one who will probably get the highest priority. With there being many voices in you, which one gets the highest priority?

This is why prayer and fasting is important. These tools enable for the right priority to be put in place. The war is the testimony of the Lord against the testimony of our flesh. The battle of the spirit against the flesh. The spirit lusts against the flesh and the flesh lusts against the spirit. Prayer and fasting determines who wins the war inside us. Prayer causes the voice and vibration of the testimony scroll of destiny in us to resonate louder. Whereas, fasting causes the voice and vibration of the testimony of the flesh to be silenced. There is one man who was talking to Jesus and he says to him, "I believe but help my unbelief". There is a dichotomy living within us. We need prayer to elevate the voice of belief and fasting to flatten the voice of unbelief. Let's overcome the seed of the enemy and crush its head by the testimony of the Lord (the seed of the woman) through the tools of prayer and fasting.

Exercise

Take out a day between 6am and 6pm to fast with no food or water. Separate yourself to worship, prayer, and reading of the Word. Then when you feel yourself at a good place in the spirit. Get a piece of paper and write down a question that you have to God about your destiny. Begin to pray in tongues for about 15 minutes. Begin to listen in your spirit. Begin to look at the screen of your mind. Take note of any words that come into your spirit. Take note of any visual pictures that come to mind. Write all that down and see what puzzle pieces of your destiny are revealed.

Chapter 10 : ASCENSION TO THE FULL SCROLL

* * *

Part of the journey of this life is to seek to know what the will of God is for our lives and aim to complete that which he has mandated for us since the beginning. Our passion must be geared in seeking to know God himself and his plans for us. This quest begins with faith to be persuaded within our heart that God has greater things for us and that we must first believe that he is and that he is a rewarder of those who seek him and his purposes. Then next, we must engage the Holy Spirit and the Lord Jesus Christ to be the guide and light to bring us to our scroll of destiny within us and unlock the scroll so we must know its contents. And from there, we must continue the process of circumcision of our hearts along with fervent prayer and consistent fasting. These types of things are the key to finding the destiny that the Father has placed in store for us. These are the types of things we can engage here on earth to look deeper within ourselves. But we must keep in mind that our God is truly the King of heaven and earth. There are some aspects left as clues for us on this earth but there are also other pieces of the puzzle that we must seek for in the heavens. The source of the original scrolls are stored in heaven. I have been in the record room in heaven and can confirm there are files with our names on it in there. Remember, that the original and primary copy is always better than the secondary copy. There are scrolls in heaven that he wants us to access that even gives a fuller picture of our responsibility as children of the Father that he wants us to fulfill. We must learn to ascend to the high places of God Almighty.

Reconciled Back to the Father

John 3

12 If I have told you earthly things, and ye believe not, how shall ye believe, if I tell you of heavenly things?
13 And __no man hath ascended up to heaven__, but he that __came down from heaven__, even the Son of man which is in heaven.

One major reason Christ died for our sins on the cross was to reconcile us back to the Father. Even for all believers and those who long for souls to come into the kingdom of God, the bible says we have the ministry of reconciliation. Since the fall of man in the garden of Eden, the Father's heart has been to be reconciled with man in spirit and in truth. This is what Christ did for us; he provided the blood to blot out the record against us that hindered us from coming boldly into the throne room of grace. Also, Christ provided the Holy Spirit that birth us again as new creations so that we can relate to the Father by the Spirit and in the spirit. This new birth brought many possibilities that we are not just beings who interact with the earth realm but now can interact with the different realms and dimensions of the spiritual realm. Jesus before he died on the cross told the disciples that he will go and prepare a place for us in his Father's house. Most think of that as something prepared for us when we die but Christ made it clear that when he prepares this place for us, he will come back for us immediately so we can be where he is. The access to the Father's house and heaven is not necessarily

131

when you die but is open for us to enter now. The Father is waiting with his arms wide open ready to welcome us back to where we came from.

As the passage above implies, Jesus in John 3, let us know there are some heavenly things besides earthly things we need to believe and understand. One of these things is that we came down here from heaven because that is our source. The goal and mission is for us to return to the source and to do this even before we die. As verse 13 shows those who came down from heaven have the ability to ascend back to heaven. Christ, the Son of God was the first and the pattern. A lot of times, we talk about the death, burial, and resurrection of Christ. We know we are to as well die to self, take up our cross, be crucified with him, be made conformable to his death, and to walk in resurrection power. But sometimes we neglect that he did not stop at resurrection, but also went on to ascension to the right hand of the Father. We are called to aspects of ascension as well. If we are to be truly "in" Christ and he is sitting at the right hand of the Father, then being in him and being where he is, means we are seated in heavenly places. There is a sound going out in the spirit from the Father to all believers saying "Come up higher" and be reconciled back to me. And when we come into awareness of the access we have to the heavens and the Father, then we can enter in and best believe he is going to show us things that will bring fullness and maturity in our lives.

Seek Those Things Above

Colossians 1 (KJV)
If ye then be risen with Christ, **seek those things which are above, where Christ sitteth on the right hand of God.**
2 **Set your affection on things above**, not on things on the earth.
3 For ye are dead, and your life is hid with Christ in God.

132

4 When Christ, **who is our life**, shall appear, **then shall ye also appear with him in glory**.

The Father and his Son, the Lord Jesus Christ, wants our awareness to also be in the higher realms of the kingdom of God. The kingdom of God is vast and covers many territories and domains. As children of the Most High, when we were born again of the spirit, now we have access to all the realms of the kingdom of God. There are levels of the heavens that we can visit and encounter. There are galaxies all over this universe that if God seems fit, you can visit. The possibilities are endless but the main thrust is that he wants you to seek him where he may be found and come where he is. The scriptures let us know two things. One is that we sit together with Christ in heavenly places (Ephesians 1). And the other is that through the resurrection of Jesus, we have been birthed again to a lively hope to an incorruptible inheritance that is reserved for us in heaven (1 Peter 1). We have to shift our mindset because many of us just think of ourselves as a physical being on earth. But the truth is that we are so much more and when we are born again, we are linked to two realms: the earth realm and the spiritual realm. In the spiritual realm, as believers we are sitting together with Christ in heavenly places but we have to awaken to that awareness. Once we come to that awareness, then we can see that there is much more waiting for us and reserved for us.

Let's now look at the verse above of Colossians 3. The heart of these 4 verses is that if we have been risen with Christ, then be filled with an affection and passion to seek those things above where Christ sits on the throne. This is not a figurative thing, this is literal and real that we are called to something higher. Some just see themselves crucified with Christ, but we have to see ourselves resurrected and ascended to the throne of the Father. This is the full message of the gospel of the kingdom. It is more than he died for us so that when we die we can go to heaven. Please know that we are supposed to now in the land of the living know him in a way that is beyond our natural minds. Apostle Paul's cry of his heart was that he may know him in the power of his resurrection. He was thinking and longing for more. There is a resurrection of the body that will occur in the end times, but there is also a resurrection and ascension of the spirit and soul that is for now. In reality, our spirit man is sitting in high places and on thrones in the high heavens. But our soul, which is the interpreter of the things of the spirit for our natural mind to comprehend, must get to a place to ascend to the place where our spirit man is connected to so it can in reality comprehend our royal position. The ascension is clear according to verse 1. Our ascension destination is sitting with Christ at the right hand of the Father. That is why Christ says you will have a seat with me on my throne.

In the Gospel According to John chapters 14 through 16, the Messiah lets us know that when he ascends to the Father, he will send the comforter which is the Holy Spirit. And after the comforter is with us, then he himself will return quickly to reveal himself to us. Most see this as the second return of Christ but it is not that. It is the revealing or should I say the revelation of Jesus Christ within you. It is him unveiling himself so you can be changed even the more and he can reconcile you to the realms of the Father. John 14:21-23, lets us know that if we obey the words of Jesus, we will be loved by him and the Father and that Jesus will manifest himself to us and from there it will lead to the Father and Son making their abode with us. We need the revelation of Jesus Christ in our hearts because as verse 4 of Colossians 3 above shows us, when Christ appears and manifests himself to us, we will appear with him in glory. This is not for later, this is for now. The revealing of Christ in us, leads us to appear with him in glory. That is why Christ is referenced to us, as Christ in us, the hope of glory. It is part of our destiny to seek those things above and ascend to the place of the Father and the Son in glory.

Inner Scroll Leads To Higher Scrolls

1 John 5 (KJV)
7 For there are three that **bear record in heaven**, *the Father, the Word, and the Holy Ghost: and* **these three are one**.
8 And there are three that **bear witness in earth**, *the Spirit, and the water, and the blood: and these* **three agree in one**.

You might wonder how all this ascension talk links to the testimony scrolls of destiny that are within us. The link is that every spiritual record on earth is connected to a record of things in heaven. The above passage shows that there are three that bear witness (record) in heaven. To bear the record is to have a testimony. And not only do these three in heaven have a testimony, the testimony is on the same page and they agree with one another. This testimony that they agree on has been written in the corridors of heaven as a number books or plethora of scrolls. The beautiful thing is that God did not just have a record or testimony in heaven but he also placed the testimony in earth as well. The Father, the Word and Holy Ghost in heaven are in alignment with the Spirit, the blood, and the water. So the parties in heaven agree with one another and there are parties on earth that agree with the testimony of the three in heaven. There are scrolls of documentation of this testimony in heaven and there are also scrolls of testimony that have been placed into man. Therefore the inward scrolls of destiny have a connection to the scrolls of testimony in heaven.

The testimony scrolls in us as humankind relates to our purposes on the earth but our destiny is so much more than what we fulfill on the earth. There are some things that he is calling for us to do in the heavenlies out of our position and authority as sitting in heavenly places with Christ. The scrolls in heaven contain a fuller record of what we are supposed to fulfill in heaven and on earth. The things of heaven are higher than the things of the earth. His ways and his thoughts are higher than our ways because he is seated higher above the heavens (the atmosphere). From an earthly mind perspective, there is so much we can reason with and understand because we are gaining information from a finite position. But when we ascend, we are doing this by our spirit man and the things revealed in the spirit while we are lifted in our spirit man unhindered by our earthly body, can be more detailed with a higher level of revelation. We in a sense, must connect the contents of our scroll within us with the knowledge of the scrolls of heaven to have the fuller picture of what we are called to do from an eternal perspective.

Heaven On Earth (The Why?)

Matthew 6 (KJV)
10 Thy kingdom come, **Thy will be done in earth, as it is in heaven**.

The above verse shows us the direction of the kingdom of God. It is the kingdom of God to originate from the position of heaven and then to manifest the substance and will of heaven into the earth. This is the summary of what we should be doing in prayer as this verse is part of the Lord's prayer. Our duties as ambassadors of heaven is to release the will of heaven into the earth so that the will of heaven can be manifested into the earth. That is why in the book of Revelation when you see the fulfillment of the kingdom of God coming into the world, we see the Lamb's wife, New Jerusalem, descending out of heaven into the earth. This shows indeed the pattern of God. It is his will for earth to be populated with the things of heaven. The goal of the kingdom is heaven on earth.

This leads us to another charge out of Matthew 6 later in the same chapter, that we should seek first the kingdom of God and his righteousness. Christ lets us know that the kingdom of God is not of this world. The disciples and other followers of Jesus were wondering why Jesus was not more of a military person at that moment to take over the kingdom of the world and restore the kingdom of Israel. His answer was that the kingdom of God is not of this world. Hence, Christ knew he had to ascend back to heaven and from that place began to send the Holy Spirit and fill the earth with the kingdom of God from the throne of heaven. Jesus Christ ascended so he can then pull down the agenda of heaven into the earth. We have to follow that same pattern. If we want to be stewards of things of the kingdom of God. We must seek the kingdom of God where the king resides. He resides not only in us but also in heaven. We must ascend to the higher place to orchestrate the manifestation of heaven on earth. This is why we ascend so we can access the scrolls of heaven to know fully what the will of God is concerning all things. And with this knowledge we can decree as sons of the Father from a place of authority into the earth. The scroll within us is there to remind of who we are but from there we must ascend to the scrolls of heaven to administer the fullness of the will of God into the earth. This is by God's design and the way of the kingdom of God.

How to Ascend?

Psalms 24 (KJV)
*3 Who shall **ascend into the hill of the Lord?** or who **shall stand in his holy place?***
*4 He that hath **clean hands**, and a **pure heart;** who **hath not lifted up his soul unto vanity, nor sworn deceitfully.***
*5 He shall receive **the blessing from the Lord**, and **righteousness from the God of his salvation.***
*6 This is **the generation of them that seek him, that seek thy face**, O Jacob.*
Selah.

We have discussed why we ascend and that is to manifest heaven into earth. But some might be questioning, how do we ascend? This is a very important question because we perish because of lack of knowledge and also for those who lack wisdom, let them ask so it can be given. Even in the Old Testament, King David in the book of Psalms was able to have a peek into the future of things that were made available to the believer in Christ. King David was a forerunner and saw many things ahead of time and he partook of things that were ahead of its time. One example is in Psalms 51, when David pleads with God to not take the Holy Spirit from him. Well the Holy Spirit was not given and made available to all until centuries later on the day of Pentecost. So how was David able to have an understanding and relationship with the Holy Spirit? It is because God granted him to step out of his time into the eternal realm where there is no time to partake of that which was already established from the beginning. So in the above Psalms 24 in verse 3, David is asking who shall ascend into the hill of the Lord or stand in his holy place? This holy place upon a hill was not a physical place but a place designated in heaven that access was not granted to everyone. This is why he said who will be able to and what qualifications will they need to have?

This also reminds me of Psalms 27, when King David iterates that there is one thing that he desires and this will he seek after. And that was that he may dwell in the house of the Lord and behold his beauty and enquire in his temple. There was not a physical temple yet so he is referring to the temple of God in heaven in the heavenly Jerusalem. There is a place that King David saw and had a glimpse and inkling of that totally turned on a passion in him. He was seeing into a future generation because in verse 6 of Psalms 24, he mentions that "this is the generation that seek him, that seek thy face". This is what it is all about in the new covenant that now Christ has opened the veil that hindered us and now we can ascend in the temple of the Lord in heaven to inquire in his temple. But we see in verse 4, that part of the how is that there are some qualifications that must be in place first.

138

Qualifications To Ascend:

- Clean Hands
- Pure Heart
- Soul Not Lifted Up in Vanity
- To Not Swear Deceitfully

The qualifications that must be in mankind to start the journey of ascension are listed above. It starts off with clean hands. We can say simply that we have to be careful what our life is touching but it is a little more deeper. Clean hands represents a priest who has clean hands in reference to a sacrifice being offered. We have been made priests of God whose aim should be to seek the temple of God in heaven. The sacrifice that leaves us bloody is the sacrifice of Jesus Christ but the priest after the brazen altar in the tabernacle then washed their hands at the brazen laver in the outer court. To have clean hands we must accept the sacrifice of Christ and be covered by his blood to forgive us our sins. From there then the washing of the water of his Word can cleans our hands for further service in his temple. From there we must have a pure heart. Notice in Psalms 51, while David was asking for the Holy spirit to stay in his life, he also asks for a clean and pure heart. This is vital. We must, as I have discussed in previous chapters, go through the process of circumcision of the heart where we are released from the wrong intents of the world and more sensitive to the things of God. Another key to ascension is that our soul should not be lifted into vanity. Our focus must be on our pursuit of God. Vanity means nothingness and idleness. We have to be careful that we are not entangled in the affairs of the world. We can't be listening, reading, talking, viewing, thinking and hearing everything that floats in this world. We must guard ourselves and stay unspotted from the world. And lastly, our vow and dedication to God must be sincere. We must let our yes to God be truly a yes from a place of sincerity, love, and passion. These alignments in our lives will make us ready to seek him so we can ascend in the heavenlies.

It all comes together as we look at verse 5, because as we seek the Father and Christ where they dwell in the heavenly temple, there is a reward there for us. He says in Hebrews 6, that without faith it is impossible to please God and he who seeks God must first believe that he is and that he is a rewarder of them that diligently seek him. There must be a determination in your heart to seek the Lord and ascend higher. The reward according to verse 5 is that we will receive the blessing of the Lord and righteousness from the God of his salvation. We are to seek the kingdom of God where the King and his throne is. But also, we are to seek his righteousness. When we come to the throne of God, there will be the blessing of the Lord which is his glory. The glory means the abundance and riches and weight and presence of God. But also, we will receive his righteousness. This blessing of glory and righteousness can only be found in its fullness before the throne of God in his holy mount and holy place. Our desire to receive all that the Father has for us and to peek into the scrolls of heaven must be also fused with the desire to seek and ascend the face of God in heaven.

Isaiah 40 (KJV)

*31 But they that **wait upon the Lord shall renew their strength**; they shall **mount up with wings as eagles**; they shall **run**, and not be weary; and they shall **walk**, and not faint.*

So our heart and our intentions must be in the right place to qualify to ascend. But also, there are a few practical things that can be done to be in position to ascend to the higher realms of the kingdom of God. Aspects of praise, worship, and prayer are very important keys to ascension. But even more important is what do you do before and after you praise, worship and pray. Before you must set in your mind a goal that you want to ascend. How can you hit a target if you are not aiming for it? You must be intentional in your seeking and asking. Now after you worship, praise, and pray, you must come to a place of stillness and wait in the presence of God. Sometimes we miss all that God wants to receive because we are in a hurry. We have to learn to set some time aside to be still in his presence and wait. When we are still, we can know that he is God. But also, being still can bring us to the place where we can see the salvation of God. The first links to Hebrews 11:6 where we first must believe that he is. Stillness and waiting brings us to that. The second links to Psalms 24:5 that in his presence we receive the righteousness of the God of our salvation. Stillness and waiting brings us to a place where we can see all the aspects that pertain to our salvation that we must walk out with fear and trembling. Waiting is so vital for us to lift up to higher places.

In Isaiah 40:3, waiting brings us to a place of strength. It also brings us to a place where we mount up with wings as eagles and run without getting weary and walk without fainting. This walking and running relates to us walking out our destiny in the world. Sometimes we run with the vision and sometimes we walk with God. The interesting thing to me I want to point out is that inside me I wondered, why did it mention mounting up with wings as eagles before it mentioned running and walking? It seems like they might have mentioned walking and running before flying. It was revealed to me that by waiting in the presence of God, that we are endowed with strength that enables us to be lifted up with wings to fly and ascend in the heavens. This causes us to view and see with vision the things that are higher and ordained for us. From that place of eagle vision, we then descend back to the earth so we can walk out and run with the vision that we received from our ascension experience. We get still and posture ourselves to wait for God to strengthen us so we can ascend to heaven to peek in and then descend to walk and run with the revelation we received. Waiting before the Lord causes us to tap into the realm of the Father and heavenly scrolls. Let's make sure we practice the art of waiting before the Lord.

What Are We Ascending To?

Hebrews 12 (KJV)

*22 But ye are come unto **mount Sion**, and unto the city of the living God, **the heavenly Jerusalem**, and to an innumerable **company of angels**,*

*23 To the **general assembly and church of the firstborn**, which are **written in heaven**, and to **God the Judge of all**, and to the **spirits of just men made perfect**,*

*24 And to **Jesus the mediator of the new covenant**, and to the **blood of sprinkling**, that speaketh better things than that of Abel.*

There is a quote by F.F. Bosworth who was a healing evangelist in the early 1900s that says "Faith begins where the will of God is known". Some might have not thought about ascending to the heavens. Some might have thought about it but did not think it was possible. I know I am just an author of this book that you might not even know, but trust me it is possible and very real. This might lead someone to want to know "what" can we see when we ascend? I can say simple, heaven and the house of God the Father himself. But I like what has been outlined in the book of Hebrews in the 12th chapter. The context is that the author of Hebrews is laying out a contrast of Moses and the children of Israel when the law of Moses was first given vs what we can now walk into. In Moses' day, there were dark clouds, lightning and thunder, a mountain that could not be touched and it was very frightening as the presence of God was revealed to the physical man in the physical plane of earth. But now that we are born of the spirit now we can arise and see and interact with the Father in spirit and truth. But starting at verse 22, it is outlined what we can engage and encounter now and it must be accessed in heaven.

• Mount Zion

- The Heavenly Jerusalem (New Jerusalem)
- Angels
- The church of the firstborn (General assembly)
- Destiny Scrolls
- Spirits of Just men made Perfect (Cloud of Witnesses)
- God the Father (the Judge of All)
- Courts and Councils of Heaven
- Jesus Christ
- The blood of the Lamb

Now the focus of this book is concerning scrolls of destiny so I won't go deep into all these categories. Hopefully in a future book I will. But I will give a quick summary because encountering all these entities or places in heaven will help and prepare you to walk in your destiny in heaven and earth. All this no matter how unbelievable it might seem is made available to all believers. The first thing I want to draw your attention to is that there is a general gathering in heaven of the church of the firstborn. The firstborn is Jesus and if you are in him, then you are part of a gathering that is happening in heaven. There have been times when I was in worship alone or corporately and I was taken to a place with other believers as we worship the Lord on one accord in the heavenlies. So there is a gathering in heaven but what is interesting to me is that it says they are written in heaven. Why did it use the word "written"? It is because it is referring to our scrolls (the books) that were written about us before the foundation of the world. It is us who are on the earth who are written about in those books and scrolls. This is why it is important to ascend so we can see the full contents of those books.

Some of the other things are Mount Zion and New Jerusalem (the heavenly Jerusalem). So we know this is not talking about physical places but spiritual places. Mount Zion is a place of kingship and sonship. It is the place we encounter to meet with King Jesus to learn more about how to reign and be a mature son of God. New Jerusalem is the city of God the Father where the holy temple of heaven is and we go there to have intimacy with Jesus and the Father to be the bride of Christ but also be priests unto God in his holy temple. Of course, to fulfill our destiny we have to work with the angels. We also will encounter the cloud of witnesses which include the saints before us who are in heaven. They will assist us and also tutor us in certain aspects concerning our destiny. The people on earth before us had destinies, mandates, and scrolls and some of them were not finished. Some did not do all their part but some it was already planned that another will do the concluding part. You have to look at it like a relay race where one person runs one leg and then hands over the baton so the other can run their leg. So the cloud of witnesses (spirits of just men made perfect) are very much vested in our activities because it was some of them who laid the foundation for us to walk in our destiny now. They are in heaven watching and cheering us on to finish the race looking to the author and finisher of our faith, Jesus Christ.

Of course, the goal will be to encounter God the Father, the judge of all and the Lord Jesus Christ in the throne room in heaven. Also, since the Father is a judge then that points to that there are courtrooms in heaven where we can enter to plead a case. Also, there are councils in heaven that regulate over certain items and territories in the earth and make judgments concerning them. But the big hurray is for the Father and Son. John 17:3 lets us know that true eternal life is to know the Father and the Son. And once again that eternal life is available now because the life is in Christ and in the Father which is housed in the eternal realm where the Father lives. We can ascend to the places and be reconciled to the Father through the blood of Jesus. Oh thank God for the blood of the Lamb and guess what the blood speaks because it has a testimony that speaks better things than Abel. It speaks better things than Abel because Abel was the son of Adam after the fall. But now we are born again to be sons of the Most High now. So we are now under the lineage of the second Adam, Jesus Christ, and now the blood is speaking awesome things for us. A better covenant with better promises. The wonders of things that God through his foreknowledge made available to us through the cross and blood of Jesus Christ. Let's arise, elevate, and ascend and let's get it!!!! Ascension allows you to access the testimony of heaven.

Relationship Breeds Responsibility and Maturity

The main point of ascension is not for the sake to say you have had all these cool experiences. But the main point is that we are called with intimacy with the Lord Jesus and the Father. There is a place in us where the Father and the Son can come and make their abode with us and manifest themselves. But the Lord Jesus and the Father have a house that is in heaven that they will like for you to come visit and dwell in at times as well. Have you ever had a friend and the relationship was all one sided? And they would come to your house all the time and eat all our food but you never went to their house, never ate a meal there, and don't even have a clue where they reside? Our heavenly Father and our wonderful savior is not calling us to that type of relationship but calling us to one of intimacy from all angles and perspectives. A relationship where there is giving from both sides. Trust and believe that God Almighty looks forward to his times with you more than you look forward than your times with him. As I like to say all the time, "Intimacy births things". In intimacy, destiny and purpose is birthed inside you. So our main focus in attempting to ascend in heaven should be intimacy. Just having the mind that you just want to be close to Him and know him to the fullest.

Then from that place of intimacy and relationship, the responsibility and maturity can be cultivated in our lives. Like in the natural realm, when a child knows their parents, it comes to a place, where the child begins to realize who they are and what their function in this family is. A father and mother sometimes have experience and an inside knowledge on what direction to guide you in and also what areas should be cultivated in your life to prepare for your destiny in the future. All this begins to unfold through fellowship, intimacy, and spending time with one another. It is that way with Jesus Christ and the Father. As we draw close, they out of the casings of relationship, begin to reveal more to us who we are and what our purpose is. There is nothing better than getting a play by play analysis and briefing about you from the one who created you. Also, besides just responsibility being revealed to us, there is also a training and preparation and transformation that is happening as we engage the Father and Son. We began to be transformed to mature and become like them in nature. This also is part of the process to prepare us for the things written on our scroll. There are things written on our scroll that depend on our ability to ascend in the heavens and access our destiny scrolls while at the same time engaging our heavenly Father so we can mature and fulfill all that is written. Ascension brings us to deeper intimacy, preparation for responsibility, and equipping and spiritual nourishment for maturity to be conformed to the image of the Son.

Exercise

Choose a day that you can carve about 4 hours where you will not be interrupted and go to a place where you will have peace and quiet. (the night time and early morning is usually the best time) First of course, repent and cover yourself with the blood of the Lamb. Choose the first half hour to worship. The next half hour, speak in tongues the whole time. The next half hour, pick certain scriptures that deal with ascension and seeking things above and begin to speak the scriptures out loud. (Even in some scriptures, put it in first person and make it personal) Then at the end, simply ask the Father, "Take me where you are so I can spend time with you" This leaves you with about 2 and a half hours left. Then pick some soaking instrumental music and play and begin to lay prostrate on the floor. Just keep your focus on the Lord and the realm of heaven while speaking no words. (Don't let your mind wander all over the place). Just sit there and wait and see if you begin to mount up with wings as eagles. Be in faith and not fear and try your best not to go to sleep. The first time, it might not happen for you but be persistent. In the waiting, even if you don't ascend right away, there will be a supernatural strength and peace that will overtake you.

Chapter 11 : WHAT IS ON OUR SCROLL? (PART 1)

* * *

The quest to reach the destination that has been ordained for our lives takes time to reach. It involves first seeking and unraveling the details of the scroll of destiny first that is within us. Also, this journey can also take a turn to bring us in the spiritual realm and into heaven to access special instructions. This journey is not for the faint of heart. It will take some resilience, persistence, patience, and of course guidance. In this journey, we need the right itinerary or map, the right mode of transportation, the right driver, pilot, or engineer, and the right fuel and power to get to the destination. There will have to be some stops sometimes to refuel and regroup but the key is to keep on pressing and never stop. We have to use the helpers and enablers of the Holy Spirit and Jesus Christ in us to assist us find and open the scroll with us. Also, we have been given the tools of prayer, fasting, tongues, mediation of the Word to circumcise our heart so we can be more discerning of the foreordained destiny given us. The question that might be burning in you since you have been reading the book probably is what is on the scrolls and books of destiny within us? I will say that the contents and details of the scroll fall into two categories. The first category is "General Calling" which pertains to the things that every man and woman who has ever been born on the earth are called to through the sacrifice of Christ. These are things that every believer shares across the board concerning their call. It is like when you are building a number of houses and all the houses have the same foundation. The second category is "Specific Calling" that pertains to the unique things that you are called to personally. It is like the fingerprint part of your scroll that nobody else can replicate. Using the house builder analogy, once you have the foundation of the house built, then the houses might differ in how many levels it has, what color it will be, how many windows, how big the yard will be and etc. The "General Calling" section and the "Specific Calling" section comes together to make a more complete picture of why the Most High God sent you out of eternity into the earth.

General Calling

2 Corinthians 5 (KJV)

*17 Therefore if **any man be in Christ**, he is a new creature: old things are passed away; behold, **all things are become new.***

*18 And all things are of God, **who hath reconciled us to himself by Jesus Christ**, and hath given to us the ministry of reconciliation;*

19 To wit, that God was in Christ, reconciling the world unto himself, not imputing their trespasses unto them; and hath committed unto us the word of reconciliation.

*20 Now then **we are ambassadors for Christ**, as though God did beseech you by us: we pray you in Christ's stead, **be ye reconciled to God**.*

The plan for mankind after the fall of man, which did not catch the Father off guard, was to repair the breach and reconcile man back to himself through the blood of Jesus Christ. It is deeper than he died for our sins so we can go to heaven when we die. We were called to be a new royal creation that would be ambassadors in the earth for the kingdom of God. To be reconciled back to Father, we have to believe in the sacrifice of Christ and be covered by the blood of the Lamb. Then our press must be to live in him so he can present and reconcile us back to the Father. The Father's desire is to be reconciled with you. This reconciliation is designed to bring you into oneness with the Father and the Son so you can be aligned to their purposes and pleasures. You become one with them and their purposes, then you take on the ministry of reconciliation to lead others to Christ so they can walk in their destiny. The general call section of your destiny scroll is linked to your reconciliation back to the Father.

The general calling section of your scroll contains functions or callings that relate to the Father, heaven, our relationship with the Father, our responsibility to the Father, and our duties as an ambassador to the kingdom of God. Everything in the general call part of the scroll is all in relation to the throne of God and our function for the Father from an eternal perspective. Through the study of the Word and through the revelation of the Holy, I have identified seven key callings or functions that are listed in the "General Calling" section of our destiny scrolls. It is interesting that the number is seven because I believe this correlates to the book (scroll) of life mentioned in the book of Revelation that contained seven seals that needed to be open. I believe in a sense the seven seals relate to the functions or callings listed in the "General Calling" section of our destiny scrolls.

Seven Seals To Unlock

Revelation 5 (KJV)
4 And I wept much, because no man was found worthy to open and to read the book, neither to look thereon.
5 And one of the elders saith unto me, Weep not: behold, the Lion of the tribe of Judah, the Root of David, **hath prevailed to open the book, and to loose the**

seven seals *thereof.*

As mentioned in a previous chapter, Jesus Christ, the Lion of Judah is the one who has triumphed and has power to unlock and loosen the seven seals of the scroll of destiny in your heart. He is a principal person to the unveiling of the scroll. It is through Christ that we are reconciled to the Father. The "General Calling" section pertains to the realm of the Father and so it is fitting that we need Jesus Christ to unlock the seals of our scroll so we can awaken to the functions we have been called to before the Father. Another note, I want to speak to is that these seals and activation into these functions and callings do not all happen at once. It is a progress and takes time and happens at the timing of the Lord Jesus Christ. Just in the parallel with the book of Revelation when Jesus Christ opened the seals. He did them one by one at different timings that released a new thing with each opened seal. This is what the seal opener is doing within us. There are seven seals of the "General Calling" that are callings from the perspective of the Eternal Father that are listed below:

1. Overcomer (Pressed and Warred To Be Reconciled with the Father)
2. Glory (Inheritance of the Father Appointed For Heirs)
3. Friend (Confidant of the Father)
4. Mature Son / Apostle (Heir & Sent One of the Father)
5. King (Reigning and Sitting With the Father & Son)
6. Priest (Minister to the Father in His Heavenly Temple)
7. Prophet (Speaker For the Father)

There is a progression that happens for us to walk in the fullness of these items on the scroll. The revealing, the maturing, and the releasing are different phases we have to take into account as well. There will be first a revealing of what the function or calling is. Then there will be a time where we have to be prepared and mature in that calling. Once we are prepared and have matured to a certain level, then the Lord Jesus Christ, will then release and anoint us in that position so we can operate more fully in that function. It is like what was always taught to me from my spiritual father, Pastor Leonard Barber. When it comes to calling, there is a calling and separation. A part when you become aware of the call and then a part where you are separated into the call. It was like in Acts 13, when Paul and Barnabas were in company with other prophets and teachers in prayer. And the Holy Spirit revealed unto them to separate Paul and Barnabas into the work and office of an apostle. The point is that before this moment, Paul in an earlier chapter of Acts knew that he called to be an apostle, but he was not separated into that call till an appointed time when he was ready. Sometimes we have to be careful because we are in a rush and in our journey of destiny we have to align with the velocity of the Father. Trust in the process and make patience your guard. Just seek to walk in all God has for you and know that as you walk , just like he did with Abraham, he will show you and unlock the seven seals of your scroll in your life. We will now take a glimpse at these seven seals.

The Overcomer

The first seal we will discuss is "The Overcomer". This is marked on everyone's scroll of destiny. This is a key reason I was told to write this book about destiny scrolls because he wants us to overcome. The fall happened. We have an enemy. We are at war. And we also have a goal, position, function, and territory that we are fighting for. The goal is to be reconciled back to the Father where he resides and dwells. We have to press and war with all our weapons to overcome and ascend to the place of salvation and redemption. We have territories and rights given to us from our Father that the enemies of God want to stifle. There are three enemies due to the fall that are there to try to stop us. They war against us everyday. These three enemies are

Satan, the world, and the flesh. Once we overcome these enemies they bring us to a realm of reconciliation to the Father.

Revelation 12 (KJV)

10 And I heard a loud voice saying in heaven, Now is come salvation, and strength, and the kingdom of our God, and the power of his Christ: for the accuser of our brethren is cast down, which accused them before our God day and night. 11 And they **overcame him by the blood of the Lamb, and by the word of their testimony;** *and they loved not their lives unto the death.*

The first enemy which is Satan wants to fight us so we don't make it fully to where we have been predestined for. And this is why the destiny scroll is important because in Revelation 12:11 (the base scripture of this book) we know that we overcome Satan, that old serpent, and the devil by the blood of the Lamb and the word of our testimony. Three things secure us victory over Satan. This might be individual wars or the whole battle. But we need the blood of the Lamb, the Word, and our testimony scroll. So the blood of Lamb that covers our sins so the accuser of the brethren can't win that legal battle is needed. We must walk in the testimony scroll given to us so we always have the goal of our destiny before us to declare in the face of the enemy. Then we must always declare the Word of God to defeat Satan like Jesus Christ did in the wilderness. He continued to tell Satan "It is written" while being tempted by Satan but won the victory. This is how you overcome the devil.

1 John 5 (KJV)

4 For whatsoever is born of God overcometh the world: and this is the victory that overcometh the world, even our faith.

The second enemy is the world. What is the world? The world is the fallen creation that we see before us that is ruled by Satan (the god of this world). The world has its own agenda and wants to keep our eyes off God the Father and on the things we see with our natural eyes. If we just look at the world in front of us, we will be blind that there is a spiritual realm. We will only consider that we are just a physical body without an eternal origin. We will continue to war with earthly and soulish weapons. This is why Christ came so we could be born again spiritually to awaken to a different reality. You must be born again to see and enter the kingdom of God. We are not to be conformed to this world but transformed into a new creation so that we can prove what is the perfect and acceptable will of God. A key to being born again and overcoming the world is faith. Faith is linked to the destiny scroll but also is a heavenly substance. Faith opens you up to a realm to see the unseen realm. Faith is not impacted by what we see in this world but it transcends and supersedes it by giving us access to the substance of things hoped for and the evidence of things not seen. It is impossible to please God without faith because you need faith to rise higher than this natural world to overcome and be reconciled back to the Father. You overcome the enemy , the world, using faith.

The third enemy keeping us from the reconciliation back to the Father and from overcoming is the flesh. After the fall, instead of living from the source of the life of God, we began to let another source and carnal nature us. The flesh has its own testimony and will that it wants to perform in your life and it continues to try the smother and silence the testimony scroll of destiny within you. The scriptures let us know that the Spirit and the flesh are at enmity and war with one another. We have to be born again and let our spirit man be joined with the Spirit of God so it can begin to rule over our soul and flesh. We want the spirit man to be king, the soul to be a servant, and the flesh to be the slave. We overcome the flesh by what is recommended in Romans 8 and that is to live by the Holy Spirit and in the spirit. We can't have two masters. It will either be the flesh or the Spirit. Choose life and be led by the Spirit of God for those will be the sons of God. We overcome the flesh by the Spirit of God. We have to defeat Satan. We have to overcome the carnal nature of our flesh and we must supersede the view and ways of this world so we can walk in the overcomer's inheritance that the Father has

154

for us.

The Glory, Our Inheritance

Ephesians 1 (KJV)

*17 That the God of our Lord Jesus Christ, **the Father of glory**, may give unto you the spirit of wisdom and revelation in the knowledge of him:*
*18 The eyes of your understanding being enlightened; that ye may know what is the hope of his calling, and **what the riches of the glory of his inheritance in the saints**,*

There are a number of scriptures that infer that when you overcome you will inherit all things. Overcoming from the bible point of view comes with an inheritance which means something you must possess as a victor or an heir. But what is this inheritance that God wants us to inherit? Simply, he wants us to inherit and possess him, the Father himself and all that he is. This inheritance is the glory of God. In Ephesians 1:17, the God of heaven and our heavenly Father is termed "the Father of Glory". This first points to that the Father of Glory must have offspring of glory as well. But it also points to what glory is. It is an attribute of the Father. It is part of his makeup and likeness. The word "of" shows that this is part of his substance and nature. The Father does not have glory because he is glory. Just like the Father is the Father of lights. He does not have light because he is light. The glory of God is himself and all his surroundings. The glory of God is the essence of heaven and God himself. The glory of the Father has many levels and dimensions to it.

There are many meanings and facets to the glory of the Father. The word glory comes from the Hebrew words "kabad" and "kabowd" which in summary between the two means to be heavy, be weighty, be grievous, be hard, be rich, be honorable, be glorious, be burdensome, be honored, weight, glory, honor, glorious, abundance, splendor, and riches. It is the revealing and unveiling of the manifest presence and person of the Father. The glory of God is the fullness of the person, nature, kingship, abundance, honor, power, and kingship of the Father. Part of the meaning of glory that might seem out of place are the words "grievous", 'hard", and "burdensome". But this makes sense because it is through tribulation and suffering that you enter into the realm of glory. The glory of the Lord is concealed and we must battle certain things to enter into the glory of the Father. That is why it is an overcomer's glory who had to overcome something in war to possess. This is what we are supposed to inherit and possess as Ephesians 1:18 shows us that the riches of the glory is the inheritance of the saints. The glory of God is the crown and the most prized possession, the Father himself, awaiting us in the final level of this video game we call life.

Romans 8 (KJV)

30 Moreover whom **he did predestinate**, them he also called: and whom he called, them he also justified: and whom he justified, **them he also glorified**.

We have been called during the process of outlining our destiny before the foundation of the world. The lamb of God was slain before the foundation of the world to justify us and even then in the past (the before), we were destined for the glory of God and this became part of the callings listed on our testimony scroll of destiny. We are called to the glory of God. There is an earthly realm. And there is a realm of the Holy Spirit. There is a realm of the Son Jesus Christ and there is a greater realm of the Father. This realm of the Father is the greatest realm and it is a realm of the greatest glory of God. This is where we are called to and we should not stop till we get there at that level. Some stop at the lowest realms and get content or think we have arrived but know if we are not operating from the position of the throne room and temple of the Father and face to face intimacy with him, then there is more to pursue and overcome. The whole pursuit is to be reconciled to the Father and the things of the realm of the Father. Jesus Christ is the reconciler, that is why he is called in us, the hope of glory. Now that Christ lives in us, we have the hope that we can enter into the glory of the Father who is the Father of glory. Besides being an overcomer, a call to the glory and realm of the Father is listed on your testimony scroll of destiny.

The Friend of God

John 15 (KJV)
*14 **Ye are my friends**, if ye do whatsoever I command you.*
*15 Henceforth **I call you not servants; for the servant knoweth not what his lord doeth: but I have called you friends**; for all things that I have heard of my Father I have made known unto you.*

There is a friendship that we can have with the Holy Spirit. There is also a friendship we can have with the Lord Jesus himself. But these friendships should lead you to the friendship with God the Father. The friendship of the Holy Spirit should lead to a friendship with the Lord Jesus because speaks and points to the Son. And our friendship with the Son will point us to the Father because the Son only speaks of the Father and acknowledges that the Father is greater. We are called on our testimony scroll of destiny to be a "Friend of God". This scroll is all from the point of view of the Father. The goal is reconciliation to the Father through Jesus Christ. Through the blood of Christ and by faith we are like a prototype and seed of Abraham that now as we believe then it will be imputed to us righteousness and we can get to a place where we are called the Friend of God (James 2:23). If we are spiritually in a sense, the seed of Abraham and he made it to that status, then we carry the DNA of that seed and it is the will of the Father that we take on that likeness, form, and traits and become a Friend of God the Father.

The scripture starting this section of John 15 in its context relates to being a friend of Jesus. But it also reveals what a friend is. In verse 15, it reveals that there is a progression that happens in serving the Father that takes you from just being a servant and becoming a friend. As a friend of God, we still have a level of obedience that he calls us to and also it does not mean that we are on the same level as him. There will still be a hierarchy where Jesus is aligned in oneness with the Father but the Father is still greater. The key indicator of being a friend of God is when you can be in a position to hear from him yourself without any other middle sources and he begins to reveal his plans and secrets to you. It is like when the Father differentiated the difference of a prophet who receives dreams and visions spiritually versus Moses who knew him face to face. Besides Abraham, I believe there were some others who had friendship with God like Moses, Elijah, and Enoch. Moses and Elijah we know that the glory of God was revealed to them. And with Elijah and Enoch, they walk so close with the Father as friends that the Father decided to translate them to stay in his realm of glory so they can be where he is.

The friend of God is when you get into a place with the Father where he delights in your presence and your conversation. It speaks to a place where he visits you and you visit him where he resides. And this visitation can progress from visitation to habitation. He begins to reveal secrets to you and brings you into what we call the secret place. You literally come into a face to face, mouth to mouth, and before the throne of God type of relationship with the Father. I love Psalms 91 that begins with "He who dwells in the secret place of the Most High shall abide under the shadow of the Almighty". This sounds pretty close to me when you come to a place where you can be in the shadow of the Most High (the Father). This place brings us to a place of rest in the shadow of the Almighty which is El Shaddai, the breasted one. In this shadow or realm of glory there is a provision, nourishment, and revealing of secrets that only comes by being a friend of God. We must let go of the world, so we are not a friend of the world and not an enemy of God. But we want to draw closer to the Father so we can be a friend of God. This was the plan of the FAther from the beginning to bring us back to a place so close to the Father and be known in all of heaven as a "Friend of God".

Prayer

Abba Father, I am thankful for those who are reading this book and hungry to press deeper to know the hope of your calling for them. As they pursue to know the contents of their destiny scrolls and as they begin to walk out there calling, let your grace be upon their lives so they can endure and finish till the end. Father, please equip them to be an overcomer over the devil, the world, and their flesh. Bring them into your realm of glory so they can walk into their overcomer's glory and wear the crown of glory appointed them in your kingdom. Also, as they draw nigh unto you, reveal yourself and usher them in your presence and your secret place so they may know you as a friend and you will know them as friends. May they walk in a close intimacy with you Father as they mature in their relationship also with the Lord Jesus Christ and the Holy Spirit. May your will, delight, and pleasure be fully formed in their lives in Jesus name. Amen.

Chapter 12 : WHAT IS ON OUR SCROLL? (PART 2)

* * *

Revelation 4 (KJV)
6 And <u>before the throne</u> there was a sea of glass like unto crystal: and in the
midst of the throne, and round about the throne, were <u>four beasts full of eyes</u>
<u>before and behind</u>.
7 And the <u>first beast was like a lion</u>, and <u>the second beast like a calf</u>, and the
<u>third beast had a face as a man</u>, and the <u>fourth beast was like a flying eagle</u>.
8 And the four beasts had each of them six wings about him; and they were full of
eyes within: and they rest not day and night, saying, Holy, holy, holy, Lord God
Almighty, which was, and is, and is to come.

In Part 1, we discussed the first three items that are listed in the "General Calling" section of the testimony scrolls of destiny that are within mankind. We are called to be an overcomer, to inherit the glory of God, and be a friend of God. There are four other callings and functions that I believe we are called to as well that we will discuss in this chapter. We still need to go a little more in depth concerning the King, the priest, mature son, and prophet callings that we must reach for in our lives. The General Calling is connected to the Father and from his perspective. In the beginning we were within him and his thoughts concerning us were from his perspective. The passage shown at the beginning of the chapter illustrates a scene of the throne room of God and the four creatures that stand before the Most High, the Father day and night. They are full of eyes which points to revelation. They walk in a closeness and a revelation of the Father that are amazing and this causes them to be in constant worship before the Father based on their intimacy with and revelation from the Father. I believe these four creatures show a parallel of what the Father is calling us to as we are reconciled back to the presence of the Father. Each creature represents a function and call that is a reflection of the nature and attributes of God the Father.

There is a spiritual law and principle that operates in the kingdom of God and probably in the demonic realm as well. This principle is that we become what we behold and based on 2 Corinthians 3:18, we change into the same image that we gaze upon. This reminds me in the first chapter of Genesis, when the Father said "Let us make men in our image and likeness". Notice this is plural in who the Father is talking about. There is a likeness of the Holy Spirit, a likeness of the Lord Jesus Christ, and also a likeness of the Father. We must engage and look upon each person of the Godhead with a face to face point of view to be changed into the same image and likeness. I believe this is what happened to the four creatures. There is another version of this scene of the throne room found in the first chapter of Ezekiel. This version insinuates that each creature displayed all the 4 faces depending on the angle you looked at them. The four faces that the four creatures are displaying is actually a reflection of the four faces of God the Father. As they continue to gaze upon the Father and his four faces, they have been changed into that same image. These four faces which represent what you see when you look at the Father represent four aspects that begin to manifest in mankind when he becomes a friend of God.

The Four Faces of the Father Realm

Faces	Function
Lion	King
Calf / Ox	Priest
Man	Mature Son (Apostle)
Flying Eagle	Prophet

The Four Faces of God Functions

From the chart, each face relates to a function and calling. The Lion relates to the King. The Calf (Ox - Ezekiel version) relates to the Priest. The Man relates to being a Mature Son and Apostle. And the flying eagle relates to the Prophet. It is interesting from an Old Testament perspective, you are able to find three types of anointings. These were times when some appointed man anointed another person by soaking them with a large amount of oil and separating them into their respective holy office. These three anointings were the kingly anointing, priestly anointing, and prophetic anointing. Also, in Genesis 1, the Most High made a pronouncement over man that they should be in his likeness and image so the face of man represents man walking in his image and likeness. The pattern for this was resonating in the Old Testament scriptures. The Father was setting a precedent of the blueprint and pattern that was setup in his Throne Room in heaven.

The other aspect I want to point out is that some might be wondering about why they see the terms prophet and apostle linked to the four faces of the Father. This is not to be confused with the apostle and prophet offices mentioned in what we call the fivefold ministry gifts (Ascension Gifts) which are apostle, prophet, pastor, teacher, and evangelist (Ephesians 4). There are three realms of the Spirit, Son, and Father that all come with their own gifts, callings, and offices. In the realm of the Spirit, we have the gifts of the Spirit and the fruit of the Spirit. In the realm of the Son (Jesus), we have the fivefold ministry gifts also known as the Ascension gifts because as he was ascending to the Father in Ephesians 4, he gave gifts to the body of Christ and church. Christ has the pre-eminence of the church and therefore his gifts are for the perfecting of the saints and equipping of the church. These gifts are not the highest level gifts and callings because he gave them while he was ascending. Also, the Father is greater than the Son. There is something higher and greater to go after. The next realm which is the realm of the Father is the highest. That is we should press toward the mark for the prize of the high calling. It is through Christ that we reach there. In the realm of the Father, the gifts are the seven spirits of God the Father and the callings are the four faces of God the Father. These callings are at a more eternal, universal, and worldwide level than the fivefold ministry gifts given by Jesus Christ. There are different levels of apostles and prophets. Some are operating from the Anointing (Jesus) level and some are operating from the Glory (Abba Father) level. The scroll's ultimate call is from the perspective being reconciled to and functioning from the Father and the Throne Room. Let's look at the functions and callings at a high level view.

The King

Revelation 1 (KJV)
6 And hath made us kings and priests unto God and his Father; to him be

glory and dominion for ever and ever. Amen.

The above verse is speaking from the perspective of what Jesus Christ through the cross allowed for us to walk into. We were made kings and priests. You don't even see kings and priests mentioned in the fivefold ministry gifts because it is reserved for God the Father. It says "kings and priests UNTO God and his Father". Jesus Christ is the King of kings and the Lord of lords. We are called to be kings and lords that are to be under the rule of the over king and overlord Jesus Christ. We are called to kingship and this was the plan from the beginning and this calling was placed on our testimony scroll that we would be joint heirs with Christ and reign with him. God the Father is the ultimate King and Jesus Christ learned kingship from the Father and we are to learn kingship from Jesus Christ and the Father. Kingship deals with thrones. Jesus ascended to the Father and sits at the right hand of the Father on a throne. As Jesus ascended he also caused us to sit with him in heavenly places on thrones because our destiny is to be kings and reign with Christ.

What does this kingship entail? Well every king has a domain in which he rules. (Even though king and son are masculine terms, this relates to men and women on the earth.) So as a king there is a set domain or given territory that God has ordained for to rule over and it should happen from the position of your throne in heavenly places. Jesus says that we have a seat with him in his throne. This speaks to the kingship we should walk in. Also, kings also war to obtain new territory or defend already attained territory. So kingship has an aspect of being a warrior. It makes sense that the lion is connected to kingship because the lion has that warrior roar. Also, kingship deals with enforcement and upholding the kingdom laws that have been decreed by the highest King. The king contains a scepter which speaks to decreeing and declaring. It is through the scepter that when a king wants to make a decree he holds the scepter and that decree stands. Also the scepter can be

164

extended to show favor or disfavor. There is a judgment side of kingship. We are called to reign, to sit, to govern, to judge, to declare, to war out the realm, authority, and power of the Father. From the position of the throne in heaven, we are to reign in heaven and earth. This is one of the seals of our scroll that must be unlocked in every believer.

The Priest

Revelation 5 (KJV)

*9 And they sung a new song, saying, **Thou art worthy to take the book, and to open the seals thereof**: for thou wast slain, and hast **redeemed us to God** by thy blood out of every kindred, and tongue, and people, and nation;*
*10 And hast made **us unto our God kings and priests:** and we shall reign on the earth.*

It is the Lord Jesus who opens the seal of our scroll and he redeems us like a preordained coupon and purchases us with a price to reconcile us back to the Father. From this redemption, we are made kings and priests unto God the Father. The Ox or Calf represents the Priest. When the husbandman is in the field or garden, he utilizes the oxen to help prepare the ground to plant seed in the earth. The oxen, which worked in pairs, would have been controlled by a yoke to be steered by a driver so the plough could overturn the earth (dirt) to bring up the nutrients so the ground can be more fertile. This is part of what a priest does. The calling is to be between the master steerer and ground so that the earth and its ways can be overturned so the ground can be fertile for the seed of the Father to produce a harvest in the earth. The priest is steered by the yoke of Jesus which yoke is easy and burden is light. It is the responsibility of the priest to be the intermediary between man and God and stand in the gap for the needs of himself and others so that aspects of the earth can be overturned to produce some new in the earth. We are called to be priests of the Father.

Another aspect of the priest and I am speaking more at a high level is their service in the temple. The Father has a temple in heaven where he is calling us to minister and serve. The priests help facilitate the sacrifice and offer the prayers and needs of the people in the temple. I believe in the throne room, the 24 elders represent the priesthood as they are the ones in Revelation 5 who are holding the prayers of the saints as a vial of odors that they present to the Father as they minister to and worship the Lord. The priest gives counsel and suggestions to the Father on behalf of the people. Prayer and Intercession are very much a part of the priesthood we are called to. The priesthood also talks of our progression of the journey we take from being not in the congregation of believers at all, to then becoming part of the congregation, then entering the gate (which is Jesus) and moving through the outer court, to the Holy Place, and then to the Holy of Holies. The Holy of Holies is where we want to end up because this is where the glory of God dwells and the Father also appears to speak to us between the cherubim. There is also an ark of covenant in there and a mercy seat which speaks about judgment. As a priest, we help legislate the things of God in the courts of heaven. The temple is linked to the courts of heaven and there are different levels of courts. The temple or tabernacle is composed of courts, the outer court, the inner court, and the holy of holies is a court as well.

This call to priesthood is a higher calling than that which we see in the Old Testament with the levitical priesthood. For this priesthood was an earthly priesthood connected to an earthly temple that showed a pattern that was showing truths to point to the heavenly temple. Jesus who came out of heaven was not a priest after the levitical priesthood but after the order of Melchizedek which is a higher order that is eternal. We are called to that same priesthood. This priesthood is a hybrid of a king and priest and it means king of righteousness. We are to be ministers of righteousness and right standing before the throne of the Father. We are to administer the blessing of the Lord through the bread of life and the new wine of the kingdom. Melchizedek is also linked to covenant as we as priests should be in covenant with Father. We should be aligning people to covenant with God and also we should be putting God the Father in remembrance of his covenant. The call of priesthood is a holy calling for we are called to a royal priesthood. This call is on the scroll for every believer to shoot for in their journey of their destiny before God.

The Mature Son & Apostle

Romans 8 (KJV)

29 For whom he did foreknow, he also did **predestinate to be conformed to the image of his Son**, that he might be the firstborn among many brethren.

The Almighty, our heavenly Father cannot be our father if he did not produce children who were after his likeness and contained his spiritual DNA. Spiritually the word "son" is used to be more in the masculine space to project things like power, authority, and strength. He is looking for more than just just something to be in his image but he is looking for us to be in his likeness. You have a child who looks like you physically, but have not matured yet or even reached adult height yet. You might have had someone who physically reached adult status but mentally is not there. Another case is someone might be a twin that looks just like you or you have a child who took on all your physical characteristics but they don't act like you or have the nature that you were trying to plant in them. Our Father is wanting us to look like him and be like him every way. In Roman 8:29, in the Father's foreknowledge, he set a destiny before we were on the earth for us to be conformed to the image of his first begotten Son who is the express image of the Father. When we see in scripture that God foreknew something, that speaks to what he placed on our destiny scroll. We are called to sonship and we have to hoist this message to the rafters and let it ring for all to hear. I often say that the message or gospel of the kingdom of God is lacking if we do not marry it with the message of sonship.

So this is why I believe one of the four faces of God that is displayed in the four living creatures is man because man was created in the image of the Father. We are to come to a place of fellowship of intimacy with the Father so it can activate his spiritual DNA in us to be transformed to the image of a son. I believe through our interaction with Jesus Christ , we learn by observation and instruction of what a son looks like. It is a discipleship, where we follow Christ and we learn his ways. But interaction with the Father is different, where something else is being activated within us. The face of the man shows that we are to become the full image of the Father expressed in heaven and earth through the Son. And by being a son since the firstborn son is the first of many brethren, we learn the Father's family business so we can be matured and take over certain parts of the business. In the realm of the Father, we are chastened and mentored as the words of the Father shape us into our full destiny. We become all that he is in nature and all that he says we are in function and purpose.

This moves us to the aspect of the apostle from the realm of the Father. This is different from the gift of Jesus to men. That gift is limited for the purpose of the church. But this calling of an apostle is from a higher plane. Apostle means a "sent one" so this speaks of coming into the realm of the Father and coming to a place of maturity where you begin to align with your eternal destiny that pertains to heaven and earth. And when the time comes that you begin to reach the mark of a mature son, you are sent from the presence of the Father with a mandate that impacts things bigger and broader than the church. The range and responsibility is bigger than just an apostle who was sent for the purpose of the church. This call of a mature son who is a sent one holds even more authority and power because you are speaking and decreeing from the position of being a ministry gift. You are speaking from the authority of being a full grown son of the Most High God. In the process when you come into the realm of the Father, there is still some chastening and tutoring that occurs. Galatians 4 says an heir is heir but in the beginning he has to depend on tutors to guide him and in the beginning he looks more like a servant. But in the realm of the Father, this is where the seven spirits of God (Father) operate to be tutors and guides to prepare, equip, and mandate you into full sonship. The call of sonship is in the "General Calling" section of the destiny scroll so we can look like our elder brother Jesus Christ and be an express image of the Father in our own way.

The Prophet

The face of the flying eagle speaks to a number of facets. It is interesting that the view of the face is not just of a face but he says it is the face of a flying eagle. It is like there is an emphasis on the flying part. This speaks to the ability to be able to ascend and fly to the highest realms of heaven which you must have to do if you are entering into the realm of the Father. Scientists say that eagles are among the company of birds that fly the highest. The eagle also is a beautiful example because this bird has a special dynamic going on with its eyes. The eyes can see from a long distance. The eyes can look into multiple directions and dimensions at once. It can be lifted up high in the air at great heights and still see its prey at ground level with great detail. I believe the eagle relates to the prophet in the realm of the Father. The prophet has great sight and can see things from a heavenly perspective and also can marry this to the perspective that it sees in the earth realm. A prophet uses that revelation to know how to navigate in the earth realm. The prophet like the eagle can fly in the air and touch the ground. The prophet at this level functions in the highest of high dimensions and can function below. The call of the prophet is on all believer's scroll.

We once again are not talking about the ministry gift function of the prophet.

169

But this functions from a different level of authority. The ministry gift of the prophet can be used to comfort, edify, exhort, predict, and bring judgment. This level deals with prophetic words within the realm of time and space. A prophet can predict things and wait for it to manifest at a certain time. But the call of the prophet from the realm of the Father deals with not per se words of prediction but words of creation. In the eternal realm of the Father, there is not the earthly perspective of time. There is no past or future, just now and the present. In this realm, all has been completed and it is a realm of rest because one aspect of the Father is that he speaks and it becomes. In this realm, the glory realm of the Father, there is a higher level of acceleration, and this type of prophet words do not fall to the ground and as soon as he or she speaks and decrees their words, it manifests right then. I believe we saw prophets like Samuel and Elijah function from this realm because they did not have the Holy Spirit functioning in their lives at that time. Samuel's words did not fall to the ground and Elijah decreed fire and rain and it manifested. This is the level of authority that this face of the Father works in us because it reflects the creative side of who he is. In the beginning, he said let there be light and light became. In this realm of the Father, the prophet does not speak from the reference of time, he speaks from the position of eternal manifestation and power that works according to the counsel of his will.

The eagle with his sight will see many things clearly. This includes the prophet seeing and knowing the will of God on many matters from an eternal perspective. The prophet will see God's eternal intention for all creation. With this knowledge, this mouthpiece for the Father, will be able to speak and release people into their purpose and offer guidance to help people get back in alignment to the preordained purposes of God. This call of the prophet will have access to the record room of heaven and begin to see the interconnections of people and their scrolls and mantles and be able to speak concerning those situations. There are many aspects of the prophet at this level and it is very powerful. He wants to work with us in these ways because he believes in us and he loves us. This is why Jesus Christ said to us, that the work he does, we will do greater because his aim was to lead us to the greater one who is the Father. And it would not just be one like it was him, it would be a many member body operating at this level of the kingdom. We are called on our scrolls of destiny to fly as an eagle as a prophet to be a mouthpiece for the Father to see from his point of view and release and create by spoken word from his point of view. We are called to great things.

The intent of this chapter was to speak to these items on the scroll at a very high level. Hopefully I will get a chance to write more books that will elaborate and expound on these with more granular detail. The truth is that we have a scroll of destiny within us that contains some items that all believers are called to and then some other items that are just for us personally. We are all called to reconcile to the Father and take on his nature and to walk in aspects and reflections of who he is. This will be manifested in us through the roles of king, priest, mature son, apostle (sent one), and prophet. All these are aspects that the Father is longing to bring forward in our lives. We have covered the seven seals that the Lord Jesus Christ wants to unlock in us so we can function at the higher level that the Father was called and predestined for us to walk in. These seals are for all believers but there are other chapters and instructions that are in scroll that only have your name on it. These can be revealed to you personally from other sources or the Father might use others who have insight on your scrolls. We have to constantly be diligent in our searching and listening to know the items of our testimony scrolls of destiny.

Prayer

Abba Father, I pray that those who are reading rise to the occasion and press to enter into the fullness of your will for their lives. Father lift them up with wings so they can rise into the realm of you where you are waiting to reveal yourself and activate them into what you have called all of us to. Bring them into an intimacy with you so that we can have a face to face relationship with you as sons. Cause them to know your throne room and serve in your heavenly temple as priests of the Most High. May they become aware of our birthright as sons of God and take their place on their thrones and reign in heaven and earth. Birth them to come in the secret place of the Almighty to mature and be sent with your mandate to release into the world from the heavens. Fill them with your wisdom and knowledge so they may open their mouths wide as a mouthpiece for you to decree and create. I ask that the seven spirits of the Father surround them to mature and make them ready for their adoption moment as a son of the kingdom of God. I ask and decree these things in their lives. In the name of Jesus Christ . Amen.

Chapter 13 : OTHER SOURCES & INDICATORS

* * *

Once again, the scroll of destiny aligned with our life and purpose has different dimensions to it. There is an aspect that outlines what we are supposed to accomplish in the earth and then what we are supposed to accomplish in the heavenly realm. There is a dimension that speaks to the temporal things we do on earth versus what we are supposed to do and what we are called to from an eternal perspective. Then the scroll is also partitioned between our general call that everyone is called to and then the items that pertain to us uniquely. These things I refer to as the "Specific Call" section of our scroll. When it comes to the "General Call" part, we can search the bible and study his word to find keys that all believers are called to. As mentioned in the previous chapters, we all are called to kingship, sonship, priesthood, the prophetic, the glory of God, friendship and reconciliation to the Father and to be overcomers. These callings are shared all through the bible when we put the pieces all together. The body of Christ or the family of God is a many-membered body whose members connect in different ways and has different functions. But the things that are specific to us, it takes a little more diligence to figure those things out. It won't be something you get all at once because it can come from other sources than just the bible. Some things will be revealed from your spiritual journey that you incur within you. Other pieces of this puzzle will come from sources outside of you. We need to learn how to tap into all these streams so we can see the full picture and end up in the full river of revelation concerning our destiny.

The Witness Within

Exodus 28(KJV)
*30 And thou shalt put in the **breastplate of judgment the Urim and the Thummim**; and they shall **be upon Aaron's heart**, when he goeth in before the Lord: and Aaron shall bear the judgment of the children of Israel upon his heart **before the Lord continually.***

Numbers 27 (KJV)
*21 And he shall stand before Eleazar the priest, **who shall ask counsel for him** after the judgment of Urim before the Lord: **at his word shall they go out, and at his word they shall come in**, both he, and all the children of Israel with him, even all the congregation.*

We all are crafted differently. We hear, see and perceive spiritual things in different ways. Some will hear words and some will see pictures, but all of them should have a part that works inside them that is able to discern things by what we feel. We need to know how to exercise the spiritual sense of feeling where we can know the direction the Lord is pulling us in even without words per se. Some will receive revelation concerning their destiny in dramatic ways that have elaborate details. And this can happen to all of us but it won't be like this all the time. We need to understand that God speaks in different modes and some are a little more subtle and not so dramatic. With Elijah he had an experience where he saw a whirlwind, then he saw a fire, but then came the still small voice. Some are looking for the wind.

Some are looking for the fire. But within there is a place where God likes to speak to us that comes from a place of stillness and peace where words are not even expressed. It is a place where you definitely have like an inside knowing or an indication of what the will of God is for you.

One of the things in the "General Call" of the believers is that we are called to be priests. Even though we called to the Melchizedek king-priest order, God provided in the Old Testament parallels and symbols of the priest side in the priesthood within the Levitical priesthood. The priests in the Old Testament wore certain garments. And part of the garment was a linen ephod. This ephod contained a breastplate that had stones on it that represented the twelve tribes of Israel but the ephod also had a place that carried two stones called the Urim and Thummim. Since this was many centuries ago, there have been different stories of exactly how these two stones operated. I have heard that it indicated a yes answer and one a no answer and when the high priest enquired of the Lord then one would glow to indicate the answer. Another version was that the stones contain etchings of Hebrew letters on them as well and that the different letters on the stones will light up to indicate a message. The whole point that this was part of the function to use these as a source to get an answer from the Almighty. Even sometimes King David will say bring the ephod to him and personally use it to enquire of the Lord for an answer. If they wanted to know if we should fight a battle or if a certain strategy was to be used, the ephod, and urim and thummim would be used. These two stones were very valuable to the priest.

I believe this shows a parallel to us as believers who are called to be priests. In one of the scriptures of this section (Exodus 28:30) we see that priests wore the urim and thummim was known as the breastplate of judgment and it positioned around the heart. This indicates that it was used to discern what was good and bad in the eyes of the Father but also it was located around the heart to reflect that this will be an inner knowing in the heart that reveals the heart of the Father. The other scripture of Numbers 27:21 reveals that it was used for counsel and that by this word of counsel is how Israel would be led in their goings and comings. This is another tool we have within us. Concerning our destiny and the scroll that is connected to our lives, we must learn how to be sensitive enough to heed the counsel of our inner urim and thummim. This is our witness within and a very effective tool to be used to know the will of God.

Sometimes it is not going to be words that come your way or a series of visions and dreams, it is going to be the witness within that you will feel either a peace, an excitement, a burden, a blockage, or a sadness. From these different, in a sense, spiritual emotions you will know and discern what is the mind and judgment of the Lord concerning your life and matter. The way it works is that you might have an opportunity that comes your way and for some reason you just have no peace about it. Every time you pray about it or think about it, you feel this yucky feeling within. This is probably an indicator that this is not for you. This makes me think of the time in the bible when Mary and Elisabeth came together and John the Baptist in the womb of Elisabeth sensed the Messiah in Mary's womb and he leaped in her womb. In a sense, John and Jesus in the beginning both had purposes and scrolls that were interwoven and when they came across one another even in the womb, both of their scrolls spoke and witnessed to one another, and John the Baptist leaped. There are times when certain people, certain words, certain scriptures, certain prophecies or certain paths before you are going to cause the spiritual baby that you are pregnant with (the scroll of destiny) in you to leap because it agrees and witnesses to the scroll within you. We must be sensitive to the witness within to know the will of God for our lives.

Weapons of our Warfare

Joel 2 (KJV)
*28 And it shall come to pass afterward, that I will pour out **my spirit upon all***

*flesh; and your sons and your daughters shall **prophesy**, your old men shall dream **dreams**, your young men shall see **visions**:*
29 And also upon the servants and upon the handmaids in those days will I pour out my spirit.

One of the main themes of this book is that we are in a war against the enemy and we need to know and fulfill our destiny to defeat him. The witness within is definitely a weapon against the enemy but there are three others I want to mention here. Those are prophecies, dreams, and visions. In the context of the scripture in Joel 2:28-29, the chapter begins with the talk of an army that the Most High will raise that is going to be very mighty and bring victory to the earth. Then later in the chapter it then reveals that the spirit of the Lord will be poured out on all flesh. To me this also points to the inner witness because we are only allowed to utilize the witness within by the Holy Spirit. Acts 1:8 lets us know that after that the Holy Ghost comes upon us, then we will have power to be witnesses. The Holy Spirit brings a witness within us and also through us to the world. But as I said before, the witness within might not be words but a feeling and sensing. So to get more details so we can know the will of God, we have been given prophecy, dreams and visions. These are manifestations and signs of the Holy Spirit being poured out on mankind. They are meant to be used for war. They are meant to be used to reveal items on our scroll.

Prophecy

Prophecy is the utterance that is given when someone speaks through the inspiration of the Holy Spirit. From the Old Testament perspective, prophesying meant to foretell events and reveal the will of God. From the New Testament perspective, prophesying means to bubble forth for the purpose of exhorting, edification, and comfort. When we put these two together, prophecy is the speaking under the influence of the Holy Spirit to edify, encourage, and comfort people that at times might foretell events. One of the calls on the general part of the scroll is to be a prophet. We are all called to be prophetic. I believe what most misunderstand is the being under the unction of God part of being prophetic. There are the revelation gifts where vision and dreams fall under and then there are inspiration or utterance gifts where prophecy falls. With revelation gifts, you either hear, see, or feel things and then begin to vocalize what you experienced. Prophesying in the true sense of the word is different. It means it bubbles forth out of you. You don't see or hear it first, it flows from you. What is being released is the first time the prophetic person and the person receiving the prophecy is hearing it. It is the person opening their mouth by faith and letting the Lord fill it with the right utterance. It is like the person tapping into a certain frequency like a radio receiver and being a conduit of the message from the source that is being transmitted. This is why visions and dreams have their own category because even though it might be prophetic in the sense that it reveals something, it is more of a two part process. The person receives information and then it processes through their mind and then they release it. Where prophecy is more one part in that it bypasses the mind and flows directly from the spirit.

This works in ways more than just talking. It works with singing. It works with dancing. It works with playing instruments. You can prophesy by actions by yielding your hands, feet, mouth, and body to the inspiration and unction of God. This is where we need to be where we are conduits of the flow of God in the earth. You might be in prayer or worship and prophecy begins to flow through you. Then you need to begin to record it down on paper or some type of audio and electronic device. You might come across someone who had a prophetic word for you that agreed with you spirit man. Then in that case you need to record it somewhere because what is being revealed at times is items that are your scroll. Knowing what is on your scroll does not happen all the time where a person sees a physical scroll before them and they can just at that one time write down the whole book. It mostly does not work like that. Sometimes we feel, see, hear, have an inner witness, and sometimes spontaneously release it into the atmosphere prophetically. Once again it comes in pieces, and we need to have our own copy where we can review the pieces that have come our way. Prophecy is one the ways God reveals to us so we can fulfill our destiny in the earth.

Dreams

Dreams are revelations that God is revealing to us while we are asleep. God uses this way because while we are asleep, our body and mind are still, and our spirit man can then reveal to us in pictures things of the spiritual realm. God is revealing but depending how close you are to him, demonic influences and even ourselves might be showing us things. I am a person who believes dreams are very important. They are revealing things about you, your surroundings, and things that God is trying to point out to you. It can give you keys about your destiny and what path you take. It can bring rebuke and also bring warning. Dreams sometimes will be literal and sometimes be cryptic by usings symbols. Nevertheless, dreams are very powerful if used the right way. Dreams sometimes come in a code and we need a code breaker to interpret these dreams. I believe a lot of times the enemy is trying to take our dreams from us so we can't decode the message of God himself that will give us the upper hand over the enemy. Dreams can reveal the items on our scroll of destiny.

It is very important to capture our dreams. Dreams are like vapors. You need to capture them before they fade away. Many of us, we wake up and we rush into our days. But if we will just slow down and begin to try to remember our dreams, then we can remember and then record them. Even if you don't know what a dream means, still record it because the interpretation or meaning might come later. There are some people who are like Daniel in the bible who have great understanding in the area of dreams. If we lack understanding of our dreams, we should find people with a good track record in this gifting and receive our interpretation. If a dream is coming to you multiple times, then it is an important message that God is trying to convey. You need to give much attention to these types of dreams. There are many types of dreams and the topic of interpretation can be very in depth and deserves the space of another book. But I want you to know that dreams are very revealing. You should have a dream journal if you can so you can see the pieces of your scroll revealed in that manner. You might not be one who dreams a lot. If so, and you want to function in this way, then begin to pray for more dreams. I am a dreamer and dreams have been a big part of my walk with God. With dreams, we have to keep everything in balance. Our main goal is to walk with God where we can hear his voice and seek his face. We can never try to just live by dreams alone because as I said some dreams can be linked to our thoughts and desires, and also if we have open doors, the enemy can come in. We must pray over every dream so we can discern the source and the message. Dreams when handled correctly can be a great source of specific items on our scroll.

Visions

Visions are like dreams in a sense but you will be awake. There are different types of visions and they can also be literal or symbolic. Visions at times if symbolic have to be interpreted as well. Also, the source of visions can be God, your own soul and imagination, and also the enemy. Visions take discernment as well and should be captured as well. There are three main categories: the inner vision, the open vision, and the trance. The inner vision is seeing things with the spiritual eye most likely with your eyes closed. The image or video will project on the screen of your mind. Open visions are when you can see images or an enactment with your physical eyes open. This may occur with you seeing most of the scenery of the room you are in and still seeing the vision. The vision screen might be so big that you don't see the scenery around you but you can still move and things like that. The trance is when your eyes are closed and your physical mobility is suspended. You are not able to move and the vision is very clear. You might be seeing within your being or you might be carried somewhere else where you are seeing the vision in another place or realm of existence. I am giving a brief summary of visions to give an idea of what they are and how they can happen. Visions even like dreams can be very helpful. If these are happening with you, then please take note as nuggets of your destiny are probably being revealed to you. And you can use these nuggets as weapons to crush the head and agenda of the enemy.

Angels

Hebrews 1 (KJV)
*7 And of the **angels** he saith, Who maketh his angels spirits, and his ministers a flame of fire.*

*14 Are they not all ministering spirits, sent forth **to minister for them who shall be heirs of salvation?***

Pertaining to the scrolls of destiny attached to our life, the role of angels is very important. While we were in the Father and all his thoughts concerning us were brewing, he through his foreknowledge knew that we would need some help when it came to fulfilling the call and destiny on our lives. So he created and manifested angels that would operate in the spiritual realm. These angels were manifested out of the Father before we came out of the Father. These angels were created to be servants and ministers first to God the Father and his royal family that carry his DNA which is us. Angels have many different posts that they are stationed at. I have seen a strategy and control center in heaven where angels receive missions and are assigned to posts. Some are stationed at the throne room, some in the atmosphere, some over some planets and stars, and some definitely on the earth. Some are even stationed even specifically to us to watch over us and help us. Some are different sizes. Some have wings and some don't. There are different classes or tribes of angels. Some carry and facilitate the glory of God. Some are appointed to the fire of God. Some are warriors that have swords, shields, and eyes of fire. I have seen these that have wings and they have muscles that look like they are bodybuilders. There even are some that will visit us in the capacity of being messengers. There are so many applications of the angels of God.

One thing that I want to share is that I was shown that for every scroll that is listed to be appropriate on the earth, there is at least one angel assigned to that scroll to watch over the scroll and assist in the fulfillment of the scroll. Depending on the weight of importance of the scroll, there might be more angels assigned to that scroll. This links to the scripture in the beginning of this section that shows that angels are ministering (serving) spirits that aid the heirs of salvation. We are the heir of salvation. Salvation goal is for us to walk in sonship to be heirs and inherit all things listed on our scroll for us to possess. Angels are very instrumental in the fulfilling of the scroll. Some might say that the angels assigned to our personal scroll are known as guardian angels. Another scripture lets us know that angels hasten to perform the word and will of God. So while we are looking to know what is on our scroll. Sometimes angels might be the source because they have inside information of our scrolls because they were assigned to our scrolls. A secret is that sometimes angels don't appear to us, they might speak to us through our spirit man and as you mature in listening spiritually you will be able to discern if it is you, the Holy Spirit, Jesus, the demonic, and even if it is angels speaking to you. Also, it is very important for us to walk according to what is on our scroll because angels will rush to assist when we are being obedient and walking in the right direction. This gives us strength and momentum in the spiritual realm to defeat the enemy because we are aligned with God. Angels are another source that can reveal aspects of the scrolls to us. It is God's intention for the family in heaven to work with the family on earth.

Seeds of Destiny

Matthew 13 (KJV)
18 Hear ye therefore the parable of the sower.
19 When any one heareth the word of the kingdom, and understandeth it not, then **cometh the wicked one, and catcheth away that which was sown in his heart.** *This is he which received seed by* **the way side.**
20 But he that received the seed into **stony places,** *the same is he that heareth the word, and anon with joy receiveth it;*
21 Yet hath he not root in himself, but dureth for a while: for **when tribulation or persecution ariseth because of the word, by and by he is offended.**
22 He also that received seed **among the thorns** *is he that heareth the word; and the* **care of this world, and the deceitfulness of riches, choke the word,** *and he becometh unfruitful.*
23 But he that received seed into the **good ground** *is he that heareth the word, and understandeth it; which also* **beareth fruit,** *and bringeth forth, some an hundredfold, some sixty, some thirty.*

There are many sources that we might receive items that are outlined on our scroll. These items we need to look at from an agriculture point of view. Every aspect of your scroll is a seed that must be planted and then watered till it produces fruit in your life. This is where the battle is because the enemy is trying to sow his seeds of tares in your heart and life. Like any other crop situation, there are bugs and weather conditions that come to destroy a crop. The bugs are the demons that the devil uses to destroy your crop and the weather conditions are storms of trials and tribulation that comes to blow the seeds of destiny from our life so there will be no fruit to harvest.

Looking at the parable of the sower, the seed that God has placed in us is the word of the kingdom. The word of the kingdom is the King's decree for your life that he wants to see manifest in your life. But as this parable goes in another version, the enemy comes immediately to steal that word. This is where the battle begins. The enemy wants to snatch the seeds of destiny right away after you come into realization of what items are in your scroll. This is the seed falling to the wayside, when the enemy is able to come right away and make you forget or turn away from the mandate on your life. Sometimes the seed of destiny might get planted, but it does not take root and when tribulation comes you get offended and let the seed die. This is the seeds of destiny falling on stony ground. Another situation is that the seeds of destiny are planted and try to grow but then the focus of us are on the world, riches, pleasures, and the cares of the world and it begins to choke the crop of destiny in our lives. This occurs because we are feeding the crop with the wrong focus. This is when the seeds of destiny are choked by the thorns of the world and the fruit does not come forth. But the ultimate of what the Lord wants to see is when we let the seed get planted, and it takes root, and the ground is good and produces fruit in different measures. This is when the seeds of destiny are good ground. It is up to you to make sure your heart is good ground.

There will always be factors of the enemy coming to snatch or choke the word of destiny in you. He always challenges the word. Satan does it in the garden in Genesis when he suggests "Did God really say that?" to cause doubt into the hearer's mind. In the wilderness when Jesus was fasting, the enemy twisted the word to try to sway the Messiah. He does not have new tricks. He is trying the same things now. We have to make sure that we are doing the right things to combat and protect the harvest of destiny that God wants to bring in our lives. We have to see the seed planted and taking root. But also, we have to make sure the seed is being fed the right nutrients in the ground that is planted in and that the seed is being watered. The right nutrients are the word of God and prayer that makes the ground of our heart fertile to produce the harvest of destiny in us. And the water is the Holy Spirit flowing through us to irrigate into our heart to cultivate the right harvest. I believe it is important to speak and pray over the things pertaining to our destiny. We must begin to take a record of the things that we know are on our scroll of destiny and begin to let the water of the words of our scroll begin to flow out our mouth and speak those things that be not, as though they were. This is what the water of the crop is doing. In the natural you might see the plant yet but know there is a seed down under and the water is going under the ground to water and calling forth the seed to rise up and manifest. We have to water the seeds of destiny by using the power of our tongue and decree them out loud as much as possible. This will scatter the enemy and attract the angels to help bring about the will of God in your life.

Putting the Scroll Together

Habakkuk 2

*2 And the Lord answered me, and said, **Write the vision, and make it plain upon tables, that he may run that readeth it.***
3 For the vision is yet for an appointed time, but at the end it shall speak, and not lie: though it tarry, wait for it; because it will surely come, it will not tarry.

We have to be like treasure hunters when it comes to our scroll and gather the pieces of this scavenger hunt. The Most High God is a God that does things line upon line, precept upon precept. That is what a book or scroll does. It outlines lines and precepts out in their set time and order to convey a full story. The key is that the vision is for an appointed time. The things on your scroll of destiny are for an appointed time. So we have to wait with patience. We don't just wait and do nothing. There is something we do while we are waiting. We must continue to write the vision of the scroll and make it plain upon the tables with as much detail we can gather. From there we have to read the vision and speak it out loud so that we can then run with the pieces of the scroll that we are supposed to run with for this season. But in the writing, waiting, reading, speaking, and running, there must be an aspect within you that believes that it will surely come. Keep the hope. Keep the faith. Keep the passion to continue to pursue the scroll's fulfillment against all odds knowing that God has given you reliable sources and strong assistance to win the war against the enemy.

What comes to my mind is the term "catch and release". This is usually used when people are fishing and they catch fish and instead of going home and cooking them, they release them back into the pond so the pond won't empty out. But in my spirit, I hear another application as it relates to the scroll of destiny in you. We have to position ourselves to "catch" the revelation of what is in the scroll, so then we can "release" that in the atmosphere so we can see the manifestation. Our words when they line up with the will of the Father are spirit and life. As we put together a tangible scroll for us to read (the catch). Then we must decree as much as possible (the release.) This is a secret to moving in our destiny because hearing it over and over again waters the seeds of destiny and causes the harvest. Speaking it over and over again activates the angels to work for you and bring you closer to the manifestation of God's destiny in your life. We have to be faithful and consistent with declaring his will over our lives. We overcome the enemy and are victorious by the blood of the Lamb and the "spoken word" of our testimony scrolls of destiny. Gather and pull together all you can of the scroll so you soar in the things that God has prepared for you.

Exercise

Get a piece of paper or open up an electronic journal or notes app. Gather together certain items from dreams, prayer times, prophetic words, and spiritual encounters that spoke to you concerning your destiny. Also include any scriptures as well that stand out and resonate strongly with you in the realm of destiny. And begin to list them in whatever order you desire. Then go through and place "I" in places to make it personal to you. in the scriptures, put the items in the first person point of view. For example, in Jeremiah 1, it states that "I have ordained you to be a prophet". So you will go through and change it on your tangible scroll as such: "God has ordained me to be a prophet to the nations". And title the list "My Scroll of Destiny". Began to recite out loud with confidence the items listed. Speak it till you begin to feel something in you come alive or until you feel his presence. Try to get in the habit of doing this as much as you can remember and also, as more gets revealed to you concerning your scroll, keep on adding and revising.

Chapter 14 : TYPES OF SCROLLS & CONCLUSION

* * *

In this book, we have mostly spoken about scrolls from a personal and individual level. But there are other scrolls that we need to be aware of as we walk this journey on the earth. Yes, the earth is filled with people. But we have to see us and other people as building blocks that build other organisms in the earth. In the garden in Genesis, eventually God said concerning Adam that it was not good that he be alone and brought Eve out of him. This means that in a world that has billions of people, we interact with each other. Our lives and our scrolls intersect with one another. We are not an island and a lot of what the Father wants to accomplish in the world comes together with us working with other people creating teams to accomplish bigger things that we could not do by ourselves. So part of the journey of fulfilling the destiny in our lives is us figuring out who we should be connected to and what team we should be playing for. Teaming up with others results in marriages, families, ministries, nations, businesses, regions, councils, organizations, and so on. Because we as individuals carry a scroll with angels assigned to us as well, then the teams and groupings of people from an eternal perspective have scrolls linked to those groupings and also a group of angels assigned to the destiny of those groupings of people. There are other scrolls besides individual scrolls of destiny and it is up to us as components of those groupings to be in tune with the plan of heaven for that grouping. God the Father in his kingdom wants to be all in all in every aspect and through his foreknowledge wrote books and scrolls concerning everything.

Families

Joshua 24 (KJV)

15 And if it seem evil unto you to serve the Lord, choose you this day whom ye will serve; whether the gods which your fathers served that were on the other side of the flood, or the gods of the Amorites, in whose land ye dwell: **but as for me and my house, we will serve the Lord.**

One of those such groupings that the Father wants to be all in all in the family unit. As the scripture right before alludes to, It is the will of the Father that the household of the family serve the Lord and do his will. Before there was a nation of Israel , a temple, a church congregation or anything you can name, the family was established in the garden before anything else. This is significant because God had purpose and destiny for the family unit. Families are the building blocks of society and the world. Families are the building block of ministries and churches. If God has destiny for families, then that means there are scrolls assigned at the family level outside of the individual level.

There is a sub component within and the family and that is the establishment of marriage. This is the pattern God intended that families will start with the institution of marriage and from there, have children to fill out the family. Then from there, create generations and a bloodline with that family. So with that breakdown, marriages have a scroll. The immediate family has a scroll and then there is a bloodline or generational scroll that the bloodline of a family is supposed to fulfill. There are angels assigned at every level and perspective. There are some angels that hang around for generations because they are assigned to a bloodline. When you begin to think of scrolls and mandates from a bigger perspective outside of just you, then it makes things more interesting. Now, you are seeking for more than just your destiny but this should make you question what is the destiny and mandate of marriage, my family and bloodline.

With marriages being the foundation of a family, it is important to make sure marriages are in alignment to the will of God. This is why we see so much divorce today because the enemy understands the importance of marriages being aligned in oneness to the destiny scroll that God ordained. I know that many don't like to look at marriage in terms of gender roles but the purpose of marriages on the earth was to be a parallel and picture of Christ's love for his body. It was to be a symbol that points to a pattern in heaven. And from the perspective of heaven, there are certain roles that are played. Christ is the husband who is the visionary and we as the bride of Christ purpose is to help him fulfill that vision. It works the same way with an earthly marriage. The husband should seek God to have a vision for his family and the wife should align with that vision and help the husband cultivate that vision.

What happens is that marriages are not following the alignment of the scroll that was assigned to them. Divorce occurs when two people are not walking as one. There is in a sense more than one vision. The oneness comes from there being one vision and that vision being aligned to the eternal purpose that God has ordained. So one thing that happens is people are not seeking God for the vision of the marriage and they are just winging it without the direction from the orchestrator up above. Another dynamic that happens is a man and a wife sometimes are coming together in matrimony out of circumstance, lust, or convenience. They are not considering their individual scrolls. If a man knows what is on his scroll while he seeks for his wife, then

190

it makes it a little easier to know who to go after. If he sees a woman and none of her traits or what she desires line up with his scroll, then this is a pretty good indicator this woman is not for him. It works in both directions. If a man approaches a woman who knows what is on her scroll and he begins to speak out his vision and it does not make the destiny baby in her leap. Then she needs to really assess if she should be with him. Another scenario is that the husband has no clue what is on his scroll and does not have a vision at all. Without a vision, the people perish. So you have a head or a priest of the home who has no clue where to go and this can lead into disaster. Tapping into the individual and marriage scrolls is crucial to the progress of a couple and family.

Eventually you might have a husband and wife and then they will have children. It is the role of the father and mother to provide a family vision to the children based on the scroll assigned to that family. It is so important to have prayer and leading from the Lord as a foundation for the family. Being tapped in the scroll of the family will help in parenting when it comes to guiding the children. Remember, each child has their own scroll and it should be the objective of the father and mother to seek items on their children's scroll. In this way, they can instruct the child in the way he should go and when the child is older they will not depart because the foundation has been laid. Knowing what is on the children's scrolls helps the parents know if they should try to develop certain talents in the child's life. It helps when it comes should they be part of certain organizations or play certain sports because you are aligning them to their destiny that through prayer God has revealed to the parents. This is by the Father's design so if it is the parent's desire to see what is on the child's scroll, the Father is willing to reveal. Seek and you shall find. The vision assigned the scrolls of the family should be before the family all the time. From this, the family can pray according to the vision and move into the destiny of the family and defeat the enemy from infiltrating their home.

Ministries / Churches

2 Chronicles (KJV)
*1 Thus **all the work that Solomon made for the house of the Lord was***
__finished__: and Solomon brought in all the things that David his father had
dedicated; and the silver, and the gold, and all the instruments, put he among the
treasures of the house of God.

Ministries and churches are other groupings that are birthed in the earth should be birthed originally in heaven in the books and scrolls of eternity. Ministries should operate based on a vision or blueprint that originated out of heaven. In 2 Chronicles, King Solomon took on the task of building a temple for the Most High in the midst of Israel. Well, Solomon did not just build a house for the LORD haphazardly but he used a blueprint of heaven that was given to his father King David. The same thing happened to Moses when he built the tabernacle. He saw a pattern out of heaven and built it according to that blueprint. Once again we see a pattern about a pattern. We need the pattern of heaven to follow to cause the end and manifestation in earth meet the beginning that is in heaven. Later in 2 Chronicles we see the fruit of King Solomon building according to God's blueprint. He did everything exactly to the design. He placed the right people in position. He placed the right items of furniture that were created in great detail in the right areas. He capped it with prayer and the result was the glory of the Most High filling the temple so much that the ministers could not stand to minister. This is the desire of the Father that we birthed things according to the scroll associated with the ministry so that it can be filled with the glory of God and cause increase. That which is born of the spirit is spirit but that which is born of the flesh is flesh.

What I was shown is that part of the problem is that there are some ministries on the earth that were not born out of heaven. But they were born out of self and some even from demonic influence. When this happens, we might see a ministry from man's perspective that seems to be thriving but on the doorpost, God has marked a sign that says "Ichabod", "The Glory Has Departed", or even worse "The Glory was never here.". Some people are just starting ministries because it was the popular thing to do or they wanted their own little kingdom to be in control over. There might be someone who is going this path because it is the family thing to do because they come from a line of pastors. When this occurs, a ministry is operating without a scroll of heaven which means there are no angels assigned specifically to that ministry. The ministry is not full of the life of God but operating in death. It is a product of flesh and the demonic to provide a counterfeit in the world that will distract others.

Another case scenario is that there is a scroll out of heaven for a ministry to be started but the person or a group of people begin to start it but they are not aligning to the scroll. Their intent is to do it another way that they have seen others do it. They are stealing from the playbook of another ministry's scroll. Because they see another minister or church has a daycare, they want a daycare. They see another emphasis is on the healing anointing, they want that to be their focus. But we must realize unless the Lord builds a house , we labor in vain. When we do things according to another ministry's scroll, that ministry is nothing but a clone ministry lacking the true heart and soul of what it was intended to be. Some ministries start off in the right direction but this detour from the scroll. They begin full of life and increase but later the glory departs. The scrolls are linked to angels and when we as ministers and leaders begin to deviate from the scroll, then the angels will be positioned there but will be limited because they are tasked to only perform God's will. Following the way of God's scroll for your ministry is vital to aligning with the kingdom of God.

I recently had a dream, while writing this book, where my wife and I went into someone else's house while they were out running errands. We were hanging out in the house and in the backyard like it was our house. We were utilizing the pool and everything. Then eventually the people came out and they were like who is this in our house. I was then told this is how a lot of people in ministry are. The Holy Spirit said, "They are not staying in their lane and desire what has been appointed to others." From this, I was reminded to be always cognizant of what is on my scroll and never leave my lane. Noah was supposed to build an ark and warn the people of the flood. He in a sense, did not get one convert but he still was aligned with the scroll and purpose of his life. Because of circumstance, we as ministers can not change lanes and try to preach and teach in areas that the anointing on our lives is not there for. May our ministries and the teaching and preaching align to God's pattern for us.

Even if we are not a leader or a founder of a ministry, we are a part of the equation. When we decide we want to attend or be a partner of a ministry, it should be according to the scroll on our lives and the right season. Some people are attending churches because their whole family attends that church. Some people have been with certain ministries for thirty plus years but that is not what their scroll says. We have to move with the cloud and direction of God and go where he leads. Because different ministries have different scrolls, sometimes your individual scroll is calling for you to be a part of different ministries only for a season. You might need healing at one place and then training at another and then eventually be in leadership at another. We can't look at how other ministries are operating. We can't look at another person if they are staying connected to a ministry for many years. Your scroll is different and we have to move according to what is written out of heaven. Once many believers look at ministries from the scroll point of view, we will see a shift in how the body of Christ operates on the earth. We would not have to worry about jealousies, schisms, and discords because everyone would understand that everyone and every ministry has their own lane. We all are supposed to walk on the highway of holiness that has many lanes.

Nations

Exodus 19 (KJV)
5 Now therefore, if ye will **obey my voice** indeed, and **keep my covenant**, then ye shall be a peculiar treasure unto me above all people: **for all the earth is mine**:
6 And ye shall be unto me a kingdom of priests, and **an holy nation**. These are the words which thou shalt speak unto the children of Israel.

Another grouping of people is on the regional or national level. People make up the population of nations. And even though all the earth is the Lords and the fullness thereof, each nation has a calling. Each nation has a mandate and a part it is supposed to play in all of creation. Certain nations are called to be leaders in industry, business, resources, military power, and righteousness. Some countries are supposed to be aligned in alliances to achieve certain things as fit by God. As shown in Exodus 19, Israel had a particular calling to be a set apart and holy nation to carry the name and ways of the Most High. Their call was even to be a treasure before God and be above in the eyes of God all people. The key was that the nation was to obey his voice and keep the covenant agreement that it had with God. The nation from the halls of heaven had a scroll assigned to it with God's plan for that nation. Every nation has a mandate that the Father wants it to fulfill.

It is the righteousness of a nation that exalts a nation but the unrighteousness that will bring judgment and reproach. There are councils that meet in heaven that discuss the affairs of the different nations in the world. From this deliberation, certain decrees and judgments are released concerning these nations. Part of the aspect of judgment that occurs is based on the scrolls linked to those nations. When a person has been called to be a prophet to the nations, they must have the ability to peek into the scrolls for those nations to effectively be the mouthpiece for God for those nations. This goes also for intercessors who intercede for world events and nations. They can't just pray whatever they want. They have to have understanding of the scrolls for those nations and also understand what is happening in the spiritual realm concerning that nation. But the scroll is the foundation for that nation and everything hinges on God's intentions and plan he ordained from the beginning through his foreknowledge.

Every scroll comes along with angels so there are ranks of angels that are assigned to every region and nation. The prophets of nations and the intercessors must work along with the angels assigned to the nations to get the will of God manifesting in their respective nations. The head angel linked to a region or nation is what we call principalities. The problem is that some principalities are aligned under the enemy. The other problem is that some countries based on the righteousness of the nation have certain judgments decreed over them and this causes certain limitations. If we want to see the full change within nations and see the glory of God fill that nation, we must begin to approach it from the mindset that there is a scroll in place and that the battle is spiritual. In this hour, I am hearing the Lord say that there are nations that he has big plans for and he is looking for his people to seek his will for those nations and begin to release the scrolls' decrees over those nations. Watch the revival and restoration to nations come into play as we align to the eternal purposes of God.

Businesses

Luke 2 (KJV)
49 And he said unto them, How is it that ye sought me? wist ye not that I must be about **my Father's business**?

196

The next grouping of people are organizations and businesses. This is another platform where people with individual scrolls come together to work as a team to accomplish certain goals and produce great services and products. Remember that every good and perfect gift comes from God above. So heaven is in the business of producing quality products and services. Some may think that everything about the kingdom of God is all about worship, prayer, and the Word but the goal is that God wants every aspect of him to impact how we operate in the earth realm. Kingdom is heaven on earth. The kingdom of God is a business and even Jesus Christ refers to the kingdom of God as his Father's business. So if from the Father's perspective, God sees his kingdom as a business and on earth we are to reflect the kingdom, then God the Father indeed has a heart for kingdom businesses to exist in the earth. If the Father is exact in every detail that relates to the human body, then through his planning and thoughts within himself, there were expected ends and scrolls concerning organizations and businesses.

Some companies are started out of greed or how much money can be made but in this hour God is called for the kingdom of God to overtake the marketplace and all its arenas. We are walking in a season where more people seeking God will end up with wisdom for witty inventions that will take the world by storm. I remember once many years ago, I was lifted up in the heavens and I saw a place where there were many technological inventions waiting for us to ascend to and take those scrolls for businesses. There are ideas that he is revealing to man that are in him from the beginning that he wants to release in the earth that will bless the earth. He needs businesses and organization to be in place because just as the family is a building block, businesses are as well. It creates a place for people with scrolls together to fulfill a common goal but also it allows for families and ministry endeavors to be supported. It is by kingdom design. Not everyone is called to marriage. Not everyone has children. Not everyone is called to be a leader of a ministry but some are called to the area of businesses and even non for profit organizations. We all have unique things that we have to fulfill individually and corporately.

I see in this hour a company of Daniels and Josephs who will be led by the Spirit of God. They will rise on the scene and they will have scrolls of destiny concerning entertainment, financial, technology, and other arenas. They will be strategically placed in companies to be a light to lead companies in the right direction with Godly counsel. Their wisdom and insight will not be of man's wisdom but supernatural as they will be able to hear and see the decrees of heaven concerning their respective companies and business endeavors. Just like Daniel was above all in wisdom concerning visions and dreams so that he was able to be an advisor to the king, God is calling Daniels in this hour. Just like Joseph, had vision and insight concerning the future of Egypt and the plan for that country in famine to be later named second in charge, God is raising up leaders like that today. The scrolls and books of heaven even have destinies outlined at the business level. Let's press in and get those ideas, witty inventions, and business scrolls from the throne room of God.

Courts of Heaven

Revelation 12 (KJV)

10 And I heard a loud voice saying in heaven, Now is come salvation, and strength, and **the kingdom of our God, and the power of his Christ**: for the **accuser of our brethren** is cast down, which accused them before our God day and night.

11 And they **overcame him** by the **blood of the Lamb**, and by the **word of their testimony**; and they loved not their lives unto the death.

It has been mentioned that there is a court of room of records in heaven that contains all the scrolls and books that were written in eternity concerning people, families, nations, businesses and other mandates. These records also work in conjunction with the courts of heaven. As we read even the two verses selected in Revelation 12, you see a scene of the courtroom if you look closely. There is the judge and king, the Father who has an advocate who is the Son. There is the enemy who is the accuser or prosecutor of the brethren and we have the witnesses and testimony of the blood of the Lamb and the Word (the will) of God. There are courts of all levels and across different realms of heaven. The enemy can not come in the highest parts of heaven so there is a court in the atmosphere (heavens) that is lower that allows him to come in and be the accuser of the brethren. This is what some refer to as the "mobile court" because the Father moves his throne on the wheels of the throne to manifest in a lower realm for court proceedings. This is very similar to the lowest levels of courts in the world that are at the municipal level. The matters of this court deals with personal interests, bloodlines, families, and other things in that arena. This is where the enemy operates because he is personally accusing you.

The enemy is accusing you based on items of the Word but also in areas that pertain to your alignment of the scroll. Because the scroll is a legal agreement that you agreed to before you came to the earth. So the enemy uses legal loopholes to come and accuse you so bad judgments can come your way. This also allows an opening for him to attack you even more because you are out of alignment of your scroll of destiny. So the enemy comes in with a case and charges based on your breaking the agreement. This is happening all the time, day and night and many of us are unaware of it. Sometimes we wonder why chaos is breaking out in our lives and the true answer is that somewhere we are out of alignment to our scroll of destiny. It is a war that the enemy is battling strategically and legally. It is like if someone was trying to defend themselves in court and didn't know the law or know the statutes and ordinances, then they will be eaten alive in court. We have to have to be acquainted with the items on our testimony scroll. We also have to value the importance of the blood of Jesus Christ and his power as a defense attorney on your behalf.

In these court proceedings, the enemy is bringing cases against violations of scrolls from your family and bloodline that might be generations old. These things have to be dealt with because the enemy will take any opportunity he can to destroy and bring curses your way. But thank the Most High for the sacrifice of Jesus Christ and his blood that can cleanse the record of our violations and our bloodlines. The blood speaks a testimony that is in your favor. The blood of Jesus and the legal services of Jesus Christ are undefeated if applied appropriately. When you go to court here on earth, the judge asks the defendant what their plea is and we usually say guilty, or not guilty and sometimes no contest. But in the courts of heaven our plea is the blood of Jesus. That is why some say, 'I plead the blood'. The courts of heaven especially the mobile court is a powerful place to be acquainted with for the believer. In this place I have had debts of 40,000 dollars supernaturally removed. Also, I had an earthly legal battle that plagued me for 7 years and by dealing with it in the courts of heaven, I received a verdict that changed my life. We have to align with the scroll of destiny and when we miss it, then we need to go back and plead the blood of Jesus so we can overcome the enemy.

The higher courts in heaven deal with nations, political items, and heavenly, eternal initiatives that need judgments. The beautiful thing about scrolls just like books is that a second or third edition can be published. The scrolls on the personal level have a general and specific calling area but there is also a revision area as well. Certain things concerning are revised based on the proceeding in the courts of heaven. Think about King Hezekiah who had a verdict that he was supposed to die by the prophet. But he repented and this made an impact in the courts of heaven and caused a revision of the judgments concerning him. Amazingly, fifteen years more of life was granted. But at first, death was his portion because he did not align to the scroll linked to his purpose and destiny. Sin means to "miss the mark". It is an archery term where we need to aim for a target but sin is to miss the target. We sometimes think of this from a moral perspective. But in reality, we can miss the mark by not fulfilling the scroll of destiny. But we must be determined to press towards the mark for the prize of the high calling in Jesus Christ. Sometimes we miss it but God in his mercy allows us to come into the courts of heaven and plead with him to bring a turn around. We can enter boldly in the courts of heaven to find favor and ask the mercy of the court. Scrolls of heaven have many implications and applications that are pertinent to life and death.

Wrap Up & Conclusion

Matthew 25 (KJV)
*23 His lord said unto him, **Well done, good and faithful servant;** thou hast been faithful over a few things, I will make thee ruler over many things: enter thou into the joy of thy lord.*

In Matthew 25, in the middle of the parable about talents, we see the Lord has given to all men different talents. Some have more than others where some have less. It was an agreed amount that was given and it was understood that he will come back later to evaluate what you did with the talents that you were given. There was one person in this example who went and hid the talent and gave it no usury and he suffered loss. But to the two others who did what they were supposed to do, they were rewarded. The Lord's words were "Well Done, good and faithful servant". He is calling all us to do well with what he has placed in us and ordained us to do. He wants us to be faithful at fulfilling the scroll of destiny and faith in our lives.

One day all of us will be before the judgment seat of God for final judgment. You might be wondering what will be the basis of this judgment. It will be based on the testimony scrolls of destiny. That will be the bar and benchmark that he will be looking at. For him to say "Well Done" means there is an expectation of the test. There is a benchmark of what was expected. The expectation is the testimony scroll of destiny. I don't want to assume but you should be asking yourselves two questions. 1) How bad do you want to hear those words, "Well done good and faithful servant"? And 2) Will you fight to overcome all to fulfill your destiny to inherit all things of the kingdom? If your answer to number 1 is "Really bad" and your answer to number 2 is "YES" emphatically, then please enter in the right relationship with Christ and the Holy Spirit so they can lead you to the contents of the scrolls of destiny uniquely fitted just for you.

The only testimony won't be just you walking in your destiny. God wants his judgment to be based on at least two or three witnesses. You will have the original witness and testimony of the Father from the beginning. You will have the Word (the Lord Jesus Christ) witness who was the express image of the Father. You have the witness of the scroll that was inside you. You will have the witness of the Holy Spirit. You will have the witness if you are a born again believer of the blood of Christ that speaks things different from Abel. You will have the witness of the life you lived. One thing I want to mention is that there is a record keeping of your life. Some angels are taking a record of everything you do, think, and say. I have seen these angels as well. So the records kept will be quite thorough. Thankfully, the power of the blood of Jesus blots out all the bad stuff through repentance. The Father is counting on us to rise to the challenge and pursue the testimony scrolls of destiny for our lives so we can also be reconciled back to him and please him in the process.

We are in the latter parts of the earth's timeline. I believe everyone who is on the earth right now agreed to come in this time. Amazing things are breaking forth in this time and our expectation should be high concerning what is coming on the scene. The world and all creation is awaiting the manifestations of the sons of God. The Father just like Jesus at the wedding has saved the best wine for last. There will be more of an awareness of the scrolls of destiny more than ever. God is revealing his truth and placing an urgency in mankind like never before to see him like never before. God the Father is such a masterful designer when it comes to his plans and the execution of them. Know that nothing catches him off guard and he has prepared for every instance and exception that can occur.

Isaiah 54 (KJV)

*17 No weapon that is formed against thee shall prosper; and every tongue that shall rise against thee in judgment thou shalt condemn. This is **the heritage** of the servants of the Lord, and **their righteousness is of me**, saith the Lord.*

There is a war and we have been predestined to win. The Father has stacked the deck and has weapons in place that the enemy has no clue about. It is like we are a sleeper agent that has a hidden agenda and programming in us that is waiting to be activated so we can do the Lord's bidding. We are the secret weapons that will defeat the enemy as well. We have the strategies and tools within us. The Father in his planning has set us up where no weapon, no matter how big or great, formed against us will not prosper. We have the right stuff. We just have to use it. Then there is a battle that happens legally in the courts of heaven because the enemy will try to raise his tongue to be against you in judgment to condemn you. But the blood of Jesus and your alignment with testimony scrolls of destiny will speak to you. You know why it will speak for you? The reason is that this is the heritage of the servants and sons of God. This has been the heritage and expectation of the family of God from the beginning since we were in the Father. The heritage is for us to overcome. The Father has overcome the enemy. Jesus Christ has overcome the enemy through the cross which gave us the blood of Christ.. Now it is our turn to defeat him through the testimony scrolls of destiny (word of our testimony). Our righteousness and right standing before the Father which is what he desires only comes from him. He had the seed of our destinies in him in eternity. Now we have to take that same testimony and become that same testimony so he can be all in all. Let's follow the instructions of the testimony scrolls and defeat the enemy in every way. The safest place during this war with the enemy is in the will of God. In his will, there is provision and overcoming strength. For where the Most High guides, he provides and protects. Know that the weapon of knowing the will of God for your life is powerful. When the enemy comes with his threats and temptations, you can tell him that "It is written" in the scrolls of eternity that I am an overcomer. The testimony scrolls of destiny should be the secret weapon that all overcomers have in their repertoire to be victorious.

About the Author

Martin Ellis, Jr. is part of the leadership team of Communion Church Ministries in the St. Louis, MO metropolitan area. He is a husband, father, songwriter, worshipper and author who has over 20 years of ministry experience as an apostolic and prophetic voice to the body of Christ. He is also known for his vibrant teaching style. He has served in areas of ministry such as prison ministry, youth pastor, worship leader, missions to Africa, and other leadership and mentoring capacities. Martin's mandate is to help others find their destinies through the grace of God. Other aspects of his mandate is to shift the body of Christ to the kingdom of God perspective, demonstrate the power of God, introduce people to the glory of God, and equip believers and leaders to flow in the move of God. He is the founder of Open Face Glory which is an outreach, internet ministry that brings focus to the kingdom, power, and glory of God. The of heart of Martin Ellis is to see the world know the supernatural working power of the Most High and see the whole earth filled with the glory of God. It is his desire for all to see Christ as King sitting on the throne of their hearts.

You can connect with me on:

🌐 http://www.openfaceglory.com

Made in the USA
Monee, IL
11 March 2021